THE
WORLD'S SIMPLEST

GUIDE TO THE STOCK MARKET

Every owner of a physical copy of this edition of

**THE
WORLD'S SIMPLEST**

GUIDE TO THE STOCK MARKET

can download the eBook for free direct from us at Harriman House, in a DRM-free format that can be read on any eReader, tablet or smartphone.

Simply head to:

**ebooks.harriman-house.com/
worldssimpleststockmarket**

to get your copy now.

THE
WORLD'S SIMPLEST

GUIDE TO
THE STOCK
MARKET

An introduction to companies,
stocks, and making money from
investing

EDWARD W. RYAN

HARRIMAN HOUSE LTD
3 Viceroy Court
Bedford Road
Petersfield
Hampshire
GU32 3LJ
GREAT BRITAIN
Tel: +44 (0)1730 233870

Email: enquiries@harriman-house.com
Website: harriman.house

First published in 2024.

Paperback ISBN: 978-1-80409-020-6
eBook ISBN: 978-1-80409-021-3

British Library Cataloguing in Publication Data
A CIP catalogue record for this book can be obtained from the British Library.

Disclosure

This material contains the current opinions of the author but not necessarily those of his employer and such opinions are subject to change without notice. This publication has been distributed for educational purposes only and should not be considered as investment advice or a recommendation of any particular security or investment product. The strategies outlined in this book may not be suitable for every individual, are not guaranteed or warranted to produce any particular results and do not contain information necessary to make investment decisions. [Consult your financial advisor or an investment professional to discuss making specific investments.]

References to specific securities and their issuers are for illustrative purposes only and are not intended and should not be interpreted as recommendations to purchase or sell such securities. The author may or may not own the securities referenced and, if such securities are owned, no representation is being made that such securities will continue to be held.

Nothing contained herein is intended to constitute accounting, legal, tax, securities, investment, or other professional advice, not an opinion regarding the appropriateness of any investment, not a solicitation of any type. Readers should be aware that all investments contain risk and may lose value. The information contained herein should not be acted upon without obtaining specific accounting, legal, tax, and investment advice from a licensed professional.

CONTENTS

PREFACE

THIS IS A concise handbook for the stock market.

In plain language, I cover everything you need to know about stocks and the stock market.

This book does not recommend or promote any specific investment strategies. Rather, it aims to provide a foundational understanding of what stocks are and how the stock market works.

WHO THIS BOOK IS FOR

There are many people across professions and experience levels who would like to better their knowledge of stocks and the stock market, but aren't necessarily looking for investment advice. That's who this book is for.

It's an ideal first read for someone new to the stock market, but it can also serve as a useful crash course for those with some experience who want or need to refresh on the basics.

A few different people in my life come to mind as examples of those who could find this book useful...

A friend of mine is a software engineer who wants to start investing, but he's never learned about stocks. Before he begins investigating different investment strategies, he'd first like to acquire an elementary understanding of what stocks are and how they trade. This book is his introduction to the stock market.

My sister works in the jewelry business, but has always had a personal interest in stocks. She also has friends and clients who work in the investment industry. I recall her once asking me if there was a book that I'd recommend to help her develop a working, conversational understanding of the stock market. This is that book.

A junior equity research analyst who, even though his job was all about stocks, entered the role as a blank slate. He took a few finance classes in college and worked a summer internship, but he was by no means an expert on the stock market. This book will help cement his foundational knowledge of stocks as he dives into deeper investment-related material.

An administrative assistant I worked with many years ago, who sat in the equities sales and trading room, wanted to better understand the language of the stock market. She wanted to know what the analysts, traders, and salespeople around her were talking about all day. This book will help.

A relative of mine has been investing his personal money for a long time. He watches CNBC every day and understands complex investment philosophies, but he jumped into investing from day one without ever learning the nuts and bolts of what stocks are and how the exchanges function. This book will help him fill in the gaps in his knowledge.

HOW THIS BOOK IS STRUCTURED

For simplicity, the book is divided into three sections: Companies, Stocks, and the Stock Market.

We start with an introduction to companies in Part One, since behind every stock there is a real company. We highlight what companies are, how they grow, and how they raise money.

We then move to stocks in Part Two. We discuss what they are, how to hold them, and how they come to be publicly listed.

Finally, in Part Three we address the stock market. We cover how stocks trade, the role of exchanges, and the historical performance of the major stock indexes, among many other topics.

The three parts are intended to flow in a way that lends itself to reading the whole book from start to finish. However, for those who wish to jump around or revisit specific sections, each part and chapter can be read independently.

As opposed to a dry, drawn-out textbook, this is meant to be a practical and accessible book. I wrote it as though I were describing the material verbally to a friend. That's how I best retain information, so that's how I relay it.

The aim here is efficiency. In the few hours it may take to read this book my hope is that you walk away with a more comprehensive understanding of stocks and the stock market.

Hope it helps.

—Ed

INTRODUCTION

THE STOCK MARKET can be a complicated subject.

Even those who interact with the market in their professional and personal lives often have glaring gaps in their knowledge.

Some individuals have most of their retirement savings invested in stocks, but they couldn't tell you what it means to be a shareholder.

Many recent college graduates with degrees in finance spent years memorizing accounting terms to pass exams, but they couldn't hold a conversation about why stock prices move.

There are probably even some professional financial advisors who invest client money in the stock market, but they'd have trouble explaining how exchanges and dark pools operate.

There is no judgement here. In my early twenties I raced into trading and investing with real money, and then later plugged in the holes in my knowledge as I learned from my mistakes, learned from colleagues, and learned from continual reading.

At some point, if you interact with the stock market in some way, it is important to develop a solid understanding of how it works.

The purpose of this book is to deliver that understanding in the most concise and easily digestible manner.

I curated the content of the book based on my own experience.

I have been thinking deeply about stocks for over 20 years in several different capacities. I have done extensive short-term trading, I am a staunch long-term investor, and I work in institutional equity sales, where I pitch stock ideas to some of the world's biggest asset managers.

When it comes to stocks, I've always asked myself: What do I need to know? What would be helpful to know? And what would I be embarrassed not to know?

It's the answers to these types of questions that determined the material in this book.

We start with companies in Part One, because you can talk stocks all you like, but if you don't understand companies, your knowledge has no grounding.

Early in my career, I remember looking closely at the price-to-earnings ratios of stocks, but I would get confused when a company talked about gross margin versus SG&A.

I would listen to CEOs and CFOs on earnings calls, but I was unclear about their relationship with the board of directors.

I understood that young companies needed to raise capital to grow, but I wasn't sure what forms it came in or who it came from.

After an introduction to companies, we move to stocks in Part Two.

Years ago, I recall buying shares of stock but not fully understanding the difference between share classes or whether I owned them in street name or direct registration.

Dividends would get deposited in my account, but I wasn't sure why some companies paid them while others prioritized share repurchases.

There were also some questions I never thought to ask myself until I was confronted with the experience, like what happens if your broker goes bankrupt?

In Part Two we also address questions like: How do analysts on Wall Street (home to the New York Stock Exchange and the financial center of the United States) estimate the value of shares? What causes share prices to move? And what's involved in the initial public offering (IPO) process?

After a thorough exploration of stocks, we move on to the stock market in Part Three.

As a young investor, I remember submitting orders to buy and sell stocks, but not knowing how or where the orders got filled. I certainly didn't understand how electronic communications networks and dark pools operated.

In this section we answer questions like: What are stock exchanges and how do they operate? How are orders submitted? How have the major stock indexes performed over time? And what are the most common ways in which individuals interact with the stock market?

Toward the end of the section, we take a brief look at options and futures. I have traded both of them. I think of them as games within the broader stock market game.

While options and futures can be complicated, and it's beyond the scope of this book to dive too deep into them, having a basic understanding of what they are and how they're used can help round out one's knowledge of stocks.

———

Truly, a lifetime could be spent studying the stock market.

If you already have experience with stocks and the stock market, this book will address the important topics where your knowledge might be lacking.

And if you are new to the subject, this book should serve as a good launching point from which you can go on to explore areas of interest in more detail. Or you can stop here, and rest assured that you have enough of an understanding to hold a conversation at your next cocktail party.

Let's get to it!

PART ONE: COMPANIES

ANY EXPLORATION OF stocks and the stock market should begin with a basic understanding of companies.

While day-to-day fluctuations in stock prices are exciting and get a lot of attention, underneath all the activity there are real companies.

Companies are businesses. They operate in different industries and promote different causes, but they all have the same aim: to generate a profit.

Their ability to do so is what ultimately determines their value.

In thinking about any company or business, there are a few things you'll want to know.

Who are the people managing the company?

How is the company's performance evaluated?

And where does the capital come from to fund the company?

These three topics—people, performance, and capital—comprise the three chapters in this part of the book.

CHAPTER 1: PEOPLE

C OMPANIES CAN SEEM like complex behemoths, but at the end of the day, they are only as functional as the people running them.

In this chapter we look at the common corporate structure in the U.S. This structure is usually formed of two tiers: the executives and the board.

The executives manage the day-to-day operations of the business, while the board ensures that the executives are doing what's in the best interest of the company's owners.

EXECUTIVES

My brother, Joey, owns and operates a food truck in Austin, Texas.

As a small business owner, he's responsible for the company's strategic decision-making, the accounting, the operations, the marketing, the human resources, and so on.

At a big company, the types of work remain the same, but it's too much for a single person to handle.

The managerial positions that are common across most big companies are not arbitrary titles. The roles reflect a logical delegation of responsibility that helps a big company function and operate efficiently.

The most common senior executive positions found at big companies are:

The **Chief Executive Officer** (**CEO**), who is the highest-ranking executive in the company. He or she is the face of the company. They typically deal with high-level strategic decisions and direct the company's overall growth strategy.

The **Chief Operating Officer** (**COO**), who oversees the day-to-day administrative and operational functions of the company. He or she typically reports directly to the CEO and is sometimes considered the second highest-ranking executive in the company.

And the **Chief Financial Officer** (**CFO**), who is responsible for managing the finance and accounting divisions of the company. He or she will track the company's financial performance, propose actions to improve it, and oversee the completion and submission of accurate and timely financial reports.

These roles are often referred to as **C-level** positions, part of what is collectively called the **C-suite**.

Some other common C-level positions include the Chief Information Officer (CIO), the Chief Marketing Officer (CMO), and the Chief Technology Officer (CTO), among several others.

When investors on Wall Street meet with a company to assess its investment prospects, they typically meet with the CEO and CFO.

The CEO is like the captain of a ship. He or she can articulate to investors where they're headed and how they plan on getting there. The CFO can back up the vision with numbers. They know how many miles they've traveled, how much fuel is in the tank, and how many people need to be on board.

Investors will also communicate regularly with a company's **Head of Investor Relations (IR)**, whose role is to manage a company's communications with the investment community.

THE BOARD

There's a lot going on at a big company.

The CEO and all his or her managers are working around the clock to grow the business. But who is overseeing all this activity and making sure it's in the best interest of the company's owners?

That's where the board comes in.

The board, also called the board of directors, is elected by the company's shareholders (owners) and is responsible for hiring and overseeing the senior management team.

The idea here is to protect shareholder interests.

In a small, family-run company, the managers of the business are also the owners, so the incentives are aligned. But when a company becomes big and its ownership is spread out among many investors who are not managing the day-to-day business, the incentives can become misaligned.

Think about it: if you invest in a company that you are not personally overseeing, who's to say the CEO that you are paying to run it won't just drain the business to fill their own pockets with cash?

That's what the two-tier corporate hierarchy system aims to protect against. The people running the business day-to-day are accountable to the board, which is in turn accountable to the shareholders.

The board is led by the **chair**, who is technically the leader of the company. He or she may also run the day-to-day affairs of the company as CEO, but in most cases the chair and the CEO are separate people. In the interest of maintaining proper checks and balances, it is usually preferable that public companies (i.e., companies whose shares are available to the public to invest in) keep these positions separate.

Some entrepreneurs understandably want to maintain complete control of their company, and perhaps in some cases their investors are happy to give it to them.

For example, at the time of this writing, Facebook founder Mark Zuckerberg serves as both the chair and the CEO of Meta.

In other cases, even rockstar entrepreneurs will cede power by forfeiting either the CEO or the chair position.

Tesla founder Elon Musk still runs his company as CEO, but he gave up the chair position. And Amazon founder Jeff Bezos did the opposite, passing on the CEO torch but maintaining the chair seat.

The chair of the board is elected by the board members.

There are two types of board members: **inside directors** and **outside directors**.

Inside directors are board members who work for the company—they have day jobs there, like the CEO, CFO, or some other senior position.

Outside directors are board members who are not employees of the company. Qualifications for outside directors vary. Companies ideally aim to have a well-rounded board made up of independent thinkers with expertise across different areas, especially finance, technology, and cybersecurity.

Public company boards need to maintain a balanced split of inside and outside directors. The purpose of having a mix of both insiders and outsiders on a company's board is to include a diversity of perspectives on how the business is being managed—specifically, if it is being managed in a way that is serving shareholder interests.

In theory, the inside directors know the company very well, but they could be biased and self-serving. Meanwhile, the outside directors aren't as close to what happens day in and day out with the business, but they offer an unbiased perspective and help ensure shareholder interests are being met.

A combination of both inside and outside directors is thought to balance the needs of the business and its owners.

In the United States, the Securities and Exchange Commission (SEC), which is an independent government agency tasked with protecting investors and maintaining fair and orderly markets, requires that company boards meet at least once per quarter.

Now we know the people who are managing and overseeing companies.

In the next chapter, we discuss how their performance in managing the business is evaluated.

CHAPTER 2:
PERFORMANCE

EXECUTIVES WILL USUALLY articulate a rosy outlook for their company.

It makes sense. Their jobs depend on them enhancing their company's performance.

So how can you judge that performance without taking the executives' word for it?

There are several basic accounting terms that are commonplace in measuring a company's performance and overall health—like revenue, expenses, earnings, cash flow, assets, and so on.

These terms make up the language of business and are important for understanding how a company's actions are translating into actual dollars of profit.

You surely don't need to be an accountant to understand the stock market, but having a general familiarity with common accounting terms will help you join the conversation.

I personally found accounting to be painfully boring when I was in school. It wasn't until I started seeing it as a numerical scorecard for real business that it became interesting.

It's like statistics in sports. If you're not a fan of basketball, then tracking points, assists, rebounds, steals, and turnovers seems meaningless.

But if you're a fan watching LeBron James try to win a championship, you realize that he's going to rack up those different stats in the process and they shed light on how he's performing.

There are three main financial statements provided by companies where most of the important numbers are highlighted. The three statements are the income statement, the balance sheet, and the cash flow statement.

Together, these three financial statements provide a numerical picture of a company's financial health and underlying value.

We'll now look at each in turn.

THE INCOME STATEMENT

A company's income statement shows how much money it gained or lost over a specific period of time.

Investors pay close attention to the income statement because it's a snapshot of how the company is performing right now.

It shows how much money the company brought in from sales versus how much money it doled out in expenses.

It can be especially useful in comparing how the company progressed from one period to the next.

A company's CEO may boast about all the promising initiatives they have in place, but if revenue has taken a big drop down versus last year, it may be cause for concern.

Whereas another company's CEO may be less of a storyteller, but if revenue is way up versus last year, they're clearly doing something right.

Table 1 is an illustration of a simple income statement.

TABLE 1: SIMPLE INCOME STATEMENT

INCOME STATEMENT PERIOD 1
Revenue
- Cost of goods sold
Gross profit
- Operating expenses
Operating income
- Non-operating income/expense
Pre-tax income
- Income tax
Net income
/ Shares outstanding
Earnings per share

The words **sales** and **revenue** are often used interchangeably. The difference is that sales refers only to the money the company receives from paying customers. Whereas revenue can include money received from other, non-operational activities like earning interest on savings or liquidating company assets.

My brother Joey's food truck sells burgers. When someone hands over a $10 bill for a burger, that's pure sales.

Generating a lot of sales is great and can be an encouraging sign of demand for a product, but the sales eventually need to translate into profit.

$1,000 in sales doesn't do Joey much good if he spent more than that on the ingredients.

The cost of the ingredients—the meat, the buns, the ketchup—are an expense. Collectively, they are referred to as the **cost of goods sold**, abbreviated as **COGS**.

The cost of goods sold includes the direct costs of producing the goods sold by a company. What's included in COGS will vary by industry. In Joey's case, it is primarily the ingredients used to create the burger, as well as the plates, napkins, and related materials.

If Joey's costs of goods sold was $400 for the day, and he made $1,000 in sales, his **gross profit** for the day would be $600.

Gross profit is the profit a company makes after deducting its direct costs (its cost of goods sold) from its revenue. It is sometimes also referred to as gross income or sales profit.

Gross profit is often considered as a percentage known as **gross margin**. The gross margin tells you what percent of the sale is profitable. In this case, for $1,000 received from burger sales, $600 of it was profit, so the gross margin was 60%.

Gross margin is important because it is the starting point for assessing the profitability of the business. If you can't sell something for more than it costs you to source the product, you may need to rethink your business model.

Unfortunately for a business, the cost of goods sold are not the only expense. There are other expenses for things like labor, rent, advertising, insurance, utilities, and office supplies. These types of indirect costs are known as **operating expenses**.

Operating expenses are business expenses that are not directly related to inventory. These items are sometimes referred to as **selling, general and administrative costs**, or **SG&A** for short.

Subtracting operating expenses from gross profit will show a company's **operating income**.

Operating income is the profit generated from core business operations. It's the money left over after accounting for the cost of the product and the costs of running the business.

The operating income expressed as percentage of sales is called the **operating margin**. The operating margin, or OP margin for short, is a useful ratio for measuring the profitability of a company's core business. It is a ratio that is closely followed by investors.

Since the OP margin is expressed as a percentage of sales rather than an absolute dollar figure, it is helpful for comparing the profitability of different companies within the same industry and measuring profitability trends over time.

For example, if Joey's operating margin is 10% but another downstreet burger truck has an operating margin of 15%, then Joey could probably do better at turning his sales into profit.

For the owners of a business, it doesn't quite end at operating income.

Things like interest payments, restructuring costs, inventory write-offs, and payments to settle lawsuits are not a direct reflection of how the underlying business is performing, but they are real expenses. It is money out of the owners' pockets.

These types of costs are considered **non-operating expenses**.

If any of these atypical activities results in a *gain* for the company, it is considered **non-operating income**.

Once a business has accounted for its non-operating expenses, it is left with **pre-tax income**.

Pre-tax income is the total amount of money made in profit before paying taxes.

But of course, the government always gets its share. After taxes are paid, that's it, you arrive at the bottom line— known as **net income**.

Net income, which is often referred to as **earnings**, is the profit left after all expenses are paid.

Earnings is the common and ultimate goal of companies. The path and time to get there varies, but the aim of all companies is to at some point generate positive earnings for their owners.

If a business only has one owner, the net income is all his or hers to keep. However, if the ownership is divided into shares of stock, as it is for publicly traded companies, then you can divide the net income by the number of shares outstanding to arrive at the earnings per share, or EPS.

EPS is an important metric for stock investors. It tells you how much of a company's earnings corresponds to each share. We will discuss EPS more in Part Two: Stocks.

THE BALANCE SHEET

The income statement gets a lot of attention because it shows how a company is performing right now, but it doesn't tell the whole story.

An army might show promise on the field, but if the country has no gold in its vaults, it may not endure.

The income statement shows the battle, but the balance sheet shows the war.

The balance sheet is a snapshot of what a company owns and owes.

Although the balance sheet can appear complex and difficult to understand, the central concept is rather simple:

Assets = Liabilities + Equity

Or put another way that might be more intuitive:

Assets – Liabilities = Equity.

Think of it like calculating your personal net worth. Take all that you own (assets), subtract all that you owe (liabilities), and you're left with your net worth (equity).

Table 2 is an illustration of a simple balance sheet.

TABLE 2: SIMPLE BALANCE SHEET

BALANCE SHEET COMPANY XYZ DECEMBER 31, 2023				
Assets		Liabilities & equity		
Current assets	Cash & cash equivalents	Current Liabilities	Accounts payable	
	Marketable securities		Accrued expenses	
	Accounts receivable		Short-term debt	
	Inventory	Long Term Liabilities	Long-term debt	
	Prepaid expenses		Other long-term liabilities	
Long-term assets	Long-term investments	Shareholder Equity	Preferred stock	
	Fixed assets		Common stock	
	Goodwill		Additional paid-in capital	
	Intangible assets		Retained earnings	
	Other long-term assets		Treasury stock	

There are whole textbooks dedicated to describing these accounting terms, so we won't go into painstaking detail on them all here, but we will address on a high level what's included in the big three buckets.

The first bucket is **assets**.

Assets

Assets include everything a company owns. They are typically broken down into current and long-term (non-current) assets.

Current assets are liquid, which means you can convert them to cash quickly if needed. These types of assets include cash and short-term investments.

When you hear that a company has a lot of cash on its balance sheet, it usually doesn't have all of it sitting around in actual cash. It might be saved in cash equivalents like money market funds that are safe but generate a small percentage return, or it might be invested in some kind of marketable security, such as government treasuries.

Current assets also includes assets that are expected to become liquid within a year, such as inventory and accounts receivable.

If your company sells T-shirts, you must have the T-shirts manufactured and delivered to you, and then you have to put them on the shelves and hope they sell. Before they do, that inventory is yours—you own it—so it's an asset on the balance sheet.

Investors in the retail space watch inventories closely because if customers don't want a company's product, it will end up having to run discounts to clear it.

Have you ever been in a store in the weeks after Christmas that had loads of Santa merchandise on clearance sale? The inventory on that company's balance sheet will likely be worth less than it had hoped.

The other group of assets is called **long-term assets**. These are things a business owns that would take longer than one year to fully turn into cash. This group includes tangible assets like property, factories, and machinery, but it also includes non-tangible assets like long-term investments and intellectual property.

The second bucket on the balance sheet is **liabilities**.

Liabilities

Liabilities include everything a company owes.

Like assets, liabilities are separated into current liabilities (those due within a year) and long-term (non-current) liabilities.

The most obvious type of liability is debt.

Debts that need to be paid soon are considered **current liabilities,** while debts with longer-maturities are considered **long-term liabilities.**

Accounts payable is a form of short-term debt where a business owes money to vendors or suppliers that have provided their business with goods or services on credit.

Quite simply, if money is owed, it is a liability and it subtracts from a company's net worth.

That leaves us with the third and final bucket on the balance sheet, **shareholder equity.**

Shareholder equity

Shareholder equity is what's left for the owners after liabilities are subtracted from assets. It's the net worth of a company on paper.

It's important to note, however, that shareholder equity is a theoretical value that only accounts for what a company owns versus what it owes without any regard to its income-generating or growth potential.

Growth prospects of course matter to the real value of a company.

Companies like Apple and Amazon are worth so much not just because their balance sheets show that the value of their buildings and cash is worth more than their debt. They are valuable because they have established tremendous businesses and brands that investors expect to generate significant earnings for a long time to come.

So, shareholder equity on the balance sheet is not the same as a company's value in the marketplace, known as **market capitalization**.

Market cap, as it's called, is the total value of all the company's shares. It's the real-time value of the company as determined by buyers and sellers of the stock.

At the end of Apple's fiscal year 2022, its balance sheet showed around $50.7 billion of shareholder equity. Its market cap at the time was over $2 trillion!

Even though shareholder equity doesn't tell you what the company is worth in the market, it is still an important gauge for the underlying health of the business.

When shareholder equity is strongly positive, it indicates that the company has sufficient assets to cover all of its liabilities. It is a country with gold in the vault, ready to endure a long war.

However, when shareholder equity is low or negative, it indicates that debts outweigh assets. If that condition persists over time, the company could face insolvency.

THE CASH FLOW STATEMENT

The final of the three critical financial statements is the **cash flow statement**.

As an individual, your tax return tells a different story than looking at the deposits and withdrawals in your bank account. It is the same with a business.

A cash flow statement provides detail on the money flowing into and out of a business during a given period. It shows how cash is being used, which is something any owner of a business should care about.

All else equal, a business that is generating a lot of cash that it can use however it wishes is better off than a company that is generating less cash.

A company's income statement might show that it had strong earnings, but it's possible they needed to spend most of the cash on maintaining property, plant, and equipment.

These types of necessary maintenance expenses are known as **capital expenditures**, or CapEx for short.

If the CapEx requirements are high, the company won't have much free cash left over to do things that investors like to see, like paying dividends, buying back shares, or reinvesting to drive future growth.

Imagine you were an investor in my brother's food truck. If he earned $50,000 last year, you would likely be happier if he told you that it's sitting in the bank and he's going to write you a check than if he told you he needed to spend it all repairing the truck and paying off a loan.

Table 3 shows a very simple example of a cash flow statement.

We will not address every term on the statement, but you will notice that it is divided into three main sections: cash flow from operations, cash flow from investing, and cash flow from financing.

Cash flow from operations shows money coming into and out of the business from regular business activities—i.e., from the main way the business makes money (by selling products, services, etc.).

Cash flow from investing shows cash earned or spent from investments the company makes, such as purchasing equipment or investing in other companies.

And cash flow from financing shows money coming into and out of the business from financing the company with loans, lines of credit, or owner's equity.

TABLE 3: SIMPLE CASH FLOW STATEMENT

CASH FLOW STATEMENT COMPANY XYZ FY ENDED DECEMBER 31, 2023	
Cash Flow from Operations	
Net Income	$100,000
Additions to Cash	
Depreciation	$20,000
Increase in Accounts Payable	$10,000
Subtractions from Cash	
Increase in Accounts Receivable	($20,000)
Increase in Inventory	($30,000)
Net Cash from Operations	$80,000
Cash Flow from Investing	
Purchase of Equipment	($5,000)
Cash Flow from Financing	
Notes Payable	$10,000
Cash Flow for FY Ended December 31, 2022	$85,000

Without getting too into the weeds, you can see from the cash flow statement that net income doesn't equal cash.

Earnings on paper do not always equal cash in the bank. Ultimately, it is cash that pays the bills.

Since business owners and investors scrutinize the use of every dollar and want to make sure there's enough cash being generated to fund the operation, the cash flow statement serves as an important complement to the income statement and balance sheet.

Taken together, the income statement, the balance sheet, and the cash flow statement provide good insight into the overall health and performance of a company.

———

Now we know how a company's performance is evaluated.

In the next chapter, we discuss a critical requirement for a company's growth—capital.

CHAPTER 3: CAPITAL

LIKE A TREE sucks water from the ground to fuel its growth toward the sky, a company needs a source of capital to expand its business.

Capital and money are somewhat interchangeable terms. The nuance is that capital is used to describe money that a company uses to fund growth. It denotes longer-term money that is being put to work for productive purposes.

Capital is also money that comes with a cost if it is raised by issuing debt or equity. Your mother might give you money for free, but an investor will charge you for capital.

FUN FACT: CAPITAL VERSUS MONEY

The word *capital* is thought to be derived from a medieval Latin term for the head, usually referring to that of cattle or other livestock.

Livestock have always been an important source of wealth and a store of value.

They represent a bridge connecting current wealth to future wealth. Livestock is a physical asset that has current value to its owner, but it is also an asset that can reproduce itself, which allows it to sustain or create surplus value over time.

Early economists such as Adam Smith, who is known as the "Father of Economics," defined capital as the part of a country's assets that initiates surplus production and increases productivity.

In a distinct contrast, the origin of the word *money* is related to the printing of currency.

Money is derived from the Latin word *moneta*, a name given to the Roman goddess Juno, at or near whose temple the Romans first began minting coins around 300 BCE.

So, when you hear capital, think of long-term wealth that produces and sustains—like cattle.

When you hear money, think of a short-term means of exchange—like coins.

SOURCING CAPITAL

Hopefully, at least some of a company's capital requirements will be generated from its own operating profit.

If a company can self-fund some of its growth through its own operations, it demonstrates that the business model is profitable and capable of sustaining the growth.

For example, it would be encouraging to see Joey open his second food truck using the profits generated from the first one.

But sometimes, especially for expensive projects, outside capital is required to move a business forward.

Think about how much money it would cost upfront to build something like an oil refinery or a steel mill. Outside capital is required to get these big projects started.

There are also instances, in a fast-paced world like ours of today, where there is simply no time to waste. When technology is disrupting industries there can be a first-mover advantage, or a winner-take-all dynamic, and the growth must happen now or never. If a company waits to expand until it is profitable, it will be too late.

For example, if the ridesharing app Uber waited to become profitable before expanding into new cities and countries, the network would have never gotten off the ground.

When Uber started disrupting the taxicab transportation market, they recognized that most of us would prefer not to have several ridesharing apps on our phone. They knew they needed to move fast to become that one ridesharing app that everyone used.

It would take time to become profitable, but they knew their idea was revolutionary and if they waited until they had sufficient profit to build out the network, some other company would come along and beat them to the chase.

Uber started in 2008 as just an idea. Within five years the founders, Travis Kalanick and Garrett Camp, had raised several hundred million dollars of private funding. By 2019, Uber had come to dominate the ridesharing market and the company was valued around $75bn. They had yet to turn a profit!

So where does the funding for growth come from, if not operating profits?

It comes in two forms: debt and equity.

A company that needs capital to grow can either borrow it (debt) or give away ownership of the company (equity) in exchange for it.

Both debt and equity investors expect a return. They're conducting business, not donating to charity.

If a company chooses to borrow money, it will have to pay interest to the lender.

If the company chooses to issue equity for money, it will be expected to generate a positive return for the new owner— maybe not immediately, but definitely at some point.

Most big companies use a combination of debt and equity funding.

Debt

Debt is a loan.

You give me money now, and I'll return it to you later along with interest. It is a pretty straightforward concept.

In the early days, a small company might take a loan from friends or family, or it might take on some credit card debt. But as a company grows bigger, it can borrow from a bank or directly from institutional investors.

Two of the main types of bank loans are installment loans and revolving loans.

With an **installment loan**, a company gets a lump sum payment up front. The loan is due to be repaid in full at some specified date in the future, and interest must be paid at regular points in the interim.

If the loan is secured, it means the company had to pledge some sort of asset as collateral. Collateral is something of value, like securities (which are tradable financial assets like stocks and bonds), real estate, or other investments that the lender is entitled to take should the company fail to make good on its promise to pay back the money and interest.

If there's no collateral pledged on the loan, it is considered unsecured.

Revolving debt is like having a credit card with a bank. A company is given a line of credit up to some specified amount that it can tap when it sees fit. The more they tap into the line of credit, and the longer they hold onto the borrowed money, the more interest they'll owe.

For bigger companies, the bank is not the only option. If there is demand, a company can issue bonds directly to investors.

A **bond** is a debt security, similar to an IOU. Companies can issue bonds to raise capital from investors who are willing to lend them money for a certain amount of time.

For example, a company might need to raise $1m in cash to fund its operations, so it could sell 1,000 bonds to the public, each with a face value of $1,000.

The individuals and investors who buy these bonds would be promised full repayment of the face value of the bond at some predetermined date in the future, called the **maturity date**. In the years leading up to the maturity date, the bond holder would receive regular interest payments.

All else equal, the more creditworthy the company, the lower the interest rate will be. The riskier the company, the higher the interest rate will be.

The interest rate compensates for risk. Intuitively, it is no different than if you were considering lending to an individual.

If a conscientious person with a stable, high-paying job wanted to borrow $1,000 from me, I wouldn't be too worried about it. I would likely lend him the money at a relatively low interest rate.

On the other hand, if a reckless gambler with a history of losing money wanted to borrow $1,000 from me, I would need to be offered a juicy deal before I agreed to it. I would need to be enticed by a high interest payment in order for me to overlook the risk, and I might want some sort of collateral pledged in case he runs away with the money. Perhaps I would hold onto his gold watch until he pays me back!

There are companies that assess the creditworthiness of corporations issuing bonds. Their aim is to help investors know whether they are lending to the conscientious worker or the reckless gambler, or someone in between.

The three most well-known bond rating companies in the U.S. are Moody's, Standard & Poor's, and Fitch. Together they account for approximately 95% of all bond ratings.

The riskiness of a company is not the only determinant of the interest rate. Time also matters.

All else equal, I would require a higher interest payment for longer time horizons. If someone wants to borrow my money for 30 years, I'll need to be compensated more than if they want to borrow it for a few days.

Short-term corporate debt with a maturity of 270 days or less is called **commercial paper**. Because of the short duration of the loan, commercial paper usually does not come with interest payments, but rather it is sold at a discount to face value. The discount to face value determines the implied rate of return for the investor.

An alternative form of corporate debt that crosses over into the world of stocks is convertible bonds. A **convertible bond** is like a regular bond in that it pays interest and has a maturity date, but it comes with a distinct feature in that it can be converted into a predetermined number of equity shares.

Convertible bonds are sometimes used by fast-growing companies with riskier financials to borrow money more cheaply than they would be able to with conventional bonds. Investors with a risk appetite may accept a lower interest rate in the hopes the equity conversion yields a handsome profit at some point in the future.

That leads us to the second bucket of funding: equity.

Equity

Equity is ownership.

In accounting terms, it is a company's assets minus its liabilities—meaning, the ownership in a company is what's left over after you add up its possessions of value (assets) and subtract all the money it owes (liabilities).

The purchasing of a house is a clear conceptual example of how equity works.

If you purchase a $1m house using a 30-year mortgage, you might pay $200,000 up front and borrow the remaining $800,000 from a bank.

You take possession of the $1m property (asset), but you owe the bank $800,000 (liability), so your equity (what you personally own) equals $200,000.

Fast forward 30 years, and you slowly but surely have paid off the entire $800,000 bank loan. You are now debt (liability) free! If the home is still valued in the market at $1m, and you have zero liability on it, then your equity is now worth $1m.

But if, to your pleasant surprise, when you decide to sell your house a buyer is willing to pay $2m for it, then the value of your equity has increased to $2m.

Equity ownership in a company follows the same concept. The debts must be paid first, but if the value of the company appreciates, so will the value of its equity.

Why do companies issue equity?

If a growing company is using cash productively to improve its business, raising too much money with debt can be burdensome. The regular interest payments can be crippling, and the looming maturity date when the whole principal of the loan is due can be disruptive.

An alternative to racking up debt can be to give away equity in the company.

By issuing equity instead of debt, the company won't be on the hook for interest payments, and it won't have a maturity date looming over it. Instead, it will just have to divvy up the ownership pie into more slices and split the profits at some point down the road. The hope is that the pie will be so much bigger that everyone will be happy with their slice.

The initial slices of ownership pie might go to friends or family, or anyone who might believe enough in the business during its infancy to give it cash.

This early group of investors might include **angel investors**, which are high-net-worth individuals who invest in early-stage companies. Angel investors can provide a capital injection in a company's early days to help get it off the ground and manage through its growing pains.

Businesses are risky bets at this early stage, but angel investors are in the high-risk/high-reward game. They typically receive equity in exchange for their cash investment. The ownership stake they receive could easily end up being worthless if the company never gains traction. But, if the company ends up becoming a huge success, the angel investor's early stake could turn into a fortune.

In 2004, an angel investor named Peter Theil invested $500,000 in a college kid's website called thefacebook.com. Over the next 15 years he ended up cashing out most of the investment for over $1 billion in profit!

As a company starts to grow and show legitimate signs of promise, it may be able to attract equity funding from venture capitalists.

Venture capital (**VC**) is similar to angel investing in that both seek to invest early in promising companies, but a VC firm typically invests a pool of investors' money. Unlike the solo angel investor who might only answer to himself, a VC firm must explain itself to clients.

VCs are expected to generate significant returns in a reasonable timeframe for their investors, so they normally look to invest in growth companies that are close to commercializing their ideas. It's still high risk/high reward, but slightly less so than angel investing.

While angel investing and venture capital are both technically forms of private equity (i.e., investment from private investors), the term *private equity* in the U.S. often refers to a specific type of private investing.

Relative to the high-growth targets of angel investors or VCs, a **private equity** (**PE**) fund will typically look to invest in more mature, well-established businesses. They are not necessarily looking for a company that is growing, but rather one that is struggling due to ineffective leadership or poor operational processes. The private equity investor will then use debt to purchase a stake in the company, attempt to make improvements to the business, and then try to sell the improved business for a profit.

Name drops: VC and PE companies

Below is a list of some of the biggest, most well-known venture capital and private equity firms in the world at the time of this writing. You may hear these names mentioned in financial media from time to time...

Venture Capital (VC) Firms

General Atlantic

Hillhouse Capital Group

Insight Venture Partners

Iconiq Capital

Tiger Global Management

Transition Level Investments

New Enterprise Associates

Norwest Venture Partners

Andreessen Horowitz

Institutional Venture Partners

Sequoia Capital

Founders Fund

Private Equity (PE) Firms

The Blackstone Group

The Carlyle Group

Kohlberg Kravis Roberts & Co. (KKR)

Thoma Bravo

CVC Capital Partners

EQT

TPG Capital

Warburg Pincus

Neuberger Berman

Leonard Green & Partners

Bain Capital

Apollo Global Management

Here is an analogy to think about these different types of investors:

The angel investor invests in an empty piece of land because they believe in its owner's vision for it.

The venture capitalist invests in a piece of land with a brand-new house already on it because they think its owner will make a fortune renting it out.

The private equity fund invests in a piece of land with a dilapidated house on it because they plan on remodeling it and flipping it for a higher price.

Now, imagine that there is a well-established hotel on the land, with a strong brand name and loyal customer following. Its owners have 100 other hotels across the East Coast of the United States, and they are confident they could add another 100 locations across the western part of the country.

To raise the capital to do it, they divide up the ownership of the company into small increments called shares of stock, and they sell the shares to the general public.

You, an individual, invest some of your savings in the shares because you think the company will generate consistent profit and help you build wealth over time.

That's the stock investor.

Now we understand companies. We've discussed what they are, who runs them, how their performance is evaluated, and how they raise money.

In the next part of the book, we move on to stocks. We will detail what stocks are, how to own them, and how they're valued.

PART TWO: STOCKS

I N THIS PART of the book we dive into stocks.

We start from square one, describing what stocks are, how they are owned, and how their owners can profit from them.

We then discuss how equity analysts assess the value of stocks, and how stocks compare to other asset classes.

Finally, we close this part of the book with an overview of the process by which a company's stock is made available to the public.

CHAPTER 4: SHARES

WHEN I WAS a kid in the 1990s, my father told me he purchased shares of Intel Corporation stock. I would turn on CNBC and watch the Intel price quote scroll by on the bottom of the screen.

I didn't really understand what it meant to own a stock, but I knew that when the price went higher, we made money, and when it went lower, we lost money.

I thought it was exciting that the price changed every time it scrolled by.

But aside from owning something that continuously fluctuates in value, what is a stock and what does it actually mean to own one?

THE BASICS

If you own a piece of gold, you can touch and feel it. You can put it on a scale and weigh it.

You can't do that with a corporation, so how can you own a piece of one?

The answer is… with stocks.

A **stock** is a security that represents ownership (equity) in a corporation.

It is a financial instrument—think of it like a virtual document—that confers legal ownership.

If you owned all of a company's stock, you would own the whole company.

Stock is a general term referring to the equity of a specific company. For example, my father owned Intel Corporation stock.

When I would watch for it on the bottom of the television screen, I would look for "INTC." This was (and still is) the company's ticker symbol.

A **ticker symbol** is a unique 2–5 letter abbreviation used to identify a stock.

The ticker symbol is usually related to the company in some way. For example, the ticker symbol for Starbucks is SBUX, the ticker symbol for Home Depot is HD, and the ticker symbol for Costco is COST.

A company's ticker symbol can be easily looked up on the internet. There are free financial databases and websites available, but a simple internet search will usually do the trick.

For example, I recently had blood drawn at Quest Diagnostics and I wondered if it was a company that had publicly traded shares of stock. A quick Google search indicated that it was indeed a public company and that its stock trades under the symbol DGX.

In my father's case, the company name (Intel) and its ticker symbol (INTC) tell you which company he owned a piece of, but not how much of it he owned.

To know that you would need to know how many units of Intel stock he owned.

An individual unit of stock is called a **share**.

A share of stock entitles its owner to a proportion of a corporation's assets and profits. It is one slice of a big pie.

Each share of stock represents an equal amount of ownership in the company. Therefore, the percent of the total available shares one owns is equal to the percent of the company one owns.

If a company has 10,000 total available shares, and you own 1,000 of them, then you would have claim to 10% of the company's assets and profits.

The total number of shares available for a given company is called its **outstanding shares**.

Anyone who owns a share of a company's stock, even if it is just one share, is considered a **shareholder**.

Stocks are priced per single share.

If you see that the price of Apple (AAPL) stock is $175, that means that at that moment one share could be bought or sold for $175.

In the example of my father, if he owned 10 shares of INTC stock, and each share was worth $25, then he owned $250 worth of stock.

If the price of each share increased to $30, then his ownership would be worth $300. Or if the price of each share fell to $20, then his ownership would be worth $200.

The price of each share will continuously change based on demand from buyers and sellers of the stock, as well changes in the amount of shares available.

OUTSTANDING SHARES ARE NOT SET IN STONE

It is important to note that the number of outstanding shares can change over time.

A company has the ability to both create new shares, which increases the total number of shares available, and to buy back and retire shares, which decreases the total number of shares available.

All else equal, when a company increases the number of shares available, it dilutes the value of the shares that previously existed. The size of the pie remains the same, but it gets divided among more slices, and your slice is made smaller.

When a company decreases the number of shares available, it enhances the value of pre-existing shares. The size of the pie remains the same, but it gets divided among fewer slices, and your slice is made bigger.

Consider the example previously noted, where a company has 10,000 total shares outstanding, and you own 1,000 of them. If the company's profits stayed the same but it decided to double its share count to 20,000, then your 1,000 shares would only entitle you 5% of the profit instead of 10%. You would be pretty mad.

Alternatively, if the company's profits stayed the same but it decided to shrink its share count by half to 5,000, then your 1,000 shares would now entitle you to 20% of the profit. You would be pleased!

Decisions to alter the share count are made by a company's board of directors, which has a fiduciary responsibility to the company's shareholders (meaning they are legally obligated to act in the shareholders' best interest). Therefore, these decisions that can fleece or enrich investors are not a result of randomness or sabotage or good luck, but rather an extension of the company's performance.

The bottom line when it comes to shares is that an investment in them is an investment in a real company. Strong companies that are consistently growing profits will find ways to enrich their shareholders, while weak companies that are struggling will lose money for their shareholders.

PRICE ISN'T EVERYTHING

Many people who are new to stocks will get caught up on the price of a stock, thinking that stocks with high share prices are expensive, while stocks with low share prices are cheap.

However, the price of a single share is not so important. It's how many shares there are in relation to how much money the company is making that determines how cheap or expensive shares really are. We address this in more detail in Chapter 7, when we discuss valuation.

For investors, what matters is the size of the total pie and the size of their slice, and those values cannot be ascertained by the stock price alone.

The concept of a **stock split** illustrates this well.

Sometimes when a company's share price becomes high, it chooses to split its shares. It does not dilute or enhance anyone's ownership, it merely restructures it.

For example, in 2022 Amazon (AMZN) decided to split its shares for the first time since the dot-com boom in 1999.

Amazon shares had enjoyed a massive two-decade long rally and climbed all the way to $2,785 per single share. To make the shares more accessible to small investors who might not be able to afford a $2,785 share, Amazon underwent a 20-for-1 stock split.

Nothing changed at the company—the amount of total sales and profit remained the same, and every shareholder's proportional ownership in the company remained the same—they simply divided each existing AMZN share into 20 new shares, each worth one twentieth of the original value.

If, before the stock split, you owned 1 share of AMZN worth $2,785, after the stock split you owned 20 shares of AMZN each worth $139.25. There was no change to the total $2,785 worth of AMZN stock that you owned, and there was no change to the percentage of the company you owned. You had exactly the same amount of pie, only it was now cut into 20 smaller slices.

A stock split like this is a simple math trick with no bearing on one's results as an investor.

It shows how irrelevant the actual price of a share can be. Amazon was the same company the day before and the day after the stock split, and owners of the stock became no richer or poorer because of it.

The only significant change is that the shares became more affordable and therefore accessible to a new cohort of investors who couldn't previously afford to invest in them.

Amazon chose to do a somewhat eye-popping 20-for-1 split because its stock had reached such a high price, but stock splits can occur in any number of ratios. The most common stock splits are 2-for-1, 3-for-2, and 3-for-1.

There are also **reverse splits**, which work in the opposite direction. In a reverse split, a company consolidates its existing low-priced shares into fewer high-priced shares.

For example, a company might announce a 1-for-5 or 1-for-10 reverse split, where investors see their five or ten low-priced shares replaced with a single higher-priced share.

A very low-priced stock, trending toward zero, can be a red flag for investors. Some exchanges will also de-list stocks that get too low in price.

For these reasons, when faced with an exceptionally low stock price, some companies will choose to do a reverse split in order to temporarily boost the per-share price of their stock.

However, they are usually not fooling anyone by the artificially juiced stock price, so news of a reverse split is often not perceived positively by investors.

TYPES OF STOCK

When people talk about owning shares of stock, they are almost always referring to **common stock**. Common stock makes up the vast majority of issued stock.

Common stock not only represents a claim on a company's assets and profits, but it also comes with voting rights.

Investors typically get one vote per share owned to elect board members. As discussed earlier, these board members hire the management team and oversee major company issues.

Individual investors who only own a small number of shares, and therefore only have a small number of votes, likely won't be too influential in corporate matters. However, big institutional shareholders who own sizeable percentages of the company's stock can exercise power over corporate policy.

Some companies issue different classes of common stock, such as Class A, Class B, and Class C shares. The primary difference between the share classes usually has to do with voting rights.

A company might choose to offer share classes with restricted voting rights if it wishes to maintain operational control of the company or make it a more difficult takeover target. If the founders or executives in the company own shares that have greater voting power than regular shares, it will make it harder for an outsider to gain enough votes to take control of the board.

Alphabet, Zillow, and News Corp., just to name a few, are examples of companies that created new classes of shares with restricted voting rights in order to preserve their owners' control over the company.

Each company can define its own share classes, so the meaning of A shares, B shares, and so on will vary.

Typically, Class A shares carry more voting rights than Class B shares. For example, a company's Class A shares might come with ten voting rights per share of stock held, while its Class B shares might offer only one vote per share. Class C shares sometimes offer no voting rights at all.

If a company offers multiple classes of shares, investors can choose which one makes sense for them.

An investor with a shorter-term mindset or one who is only concerned with the share price might be fine to purchase a class of shares with no voting rights. Whereas an investor who wants to be active in corporate governance might place emphasis on owning the class of shares that confers the most votes.

Even though the different share classes represent ownership in the same company, they can deviate in performance based on demand for the shares. Historically, Class A shares have tended to slightly outperform other share classes, but that does not always have to be the case.

Most companies do *not* offer multiple classes of stock, so as an individual investor this is something to be aware of but not something to fret over.

You can tell if a company offers more than one share class to the public if there are slightly different ticker symbols available for the same company stock.

For example, Alphabet offers GOOGL (Class A) shares and GOOG (Class C) shares, Zillow Group offers ZG (Class A) shares and Z (Class C) shares, and News Corp. offers NWSA (Class A) and NWS (Class B) shares.

If you were to pull up price charts of the competing shares, you would notice that the price of the shares might differ slightly, but the performance is directionally the same.

LIABILITY

When I started investing in common shares, I remember asking myself: what happens if the company does something illegal and gets sued? Would I be financially liable?

The answer is no.

Public companies are set up as **corporations**, which is a legal structure that deems the corporation as separate from its owners.

Essentially, the corporation is its own entity, and the owners of it are—collectively—another.

This is a critical distinction because it means that investors in the corporation are not legally responsible for the actions or debts of the company.

Investors can lose the entire amount of their investment, but no more than that.

If individual investors were on the hook for potentially limitless losses due to lawsuits or company mismanagement, the risk-reward proposition of investing probably wouldn't make sense.

In fact, before the introduction of limited liability laws, very few people invested their personal money in stocks.

The world's first modern limited liability law was enacted by the state of New York in 1811. It originally only applied to manufacturing companies, but its enactment resulted in companies locating there from other states. Eventually every state followed New York's lead and the concept was applied across industries.

The limited liability standard was a fundamental step in securities law and was a catalyst for greater adoption of stock investing in the United States and elsewhere.

PREFERRED STOCK

Common stock, including all its possible share classes, is the most widely issued and owned type of stock. If you turn on financial media and they are talking about stocks, they are almost always referring to common stocks.

The other type of stock is **preferred stock**.

Preferred stock is in some respects closer to bonds than it is to common stock. While preferred shares do entitle the holder to equity in the company, they also pay regular interest or dividends based on the **par value** of the asset—like a bond.

Par value, also called **face value** or **nominal value**, is the stated value of a security (i.e., a financial asset). It's what's printed on the bond certificate when the company first issues it.

Bonds, for example, are usually issued with a maturity date, a stated interest rate, and par value of $1,000.

If a company issues a 10-year bond with a 5% interest rate and a $1,000 par value, that means the buyer of the bond will receive their $1,000 back at the end of ten years, while receiving 5% annual interest payments in the interim.

In the case of common stocks, the par value is of little significance to the owner. It is an arbitrary value assigned for balance sheet purposes when the company issues shares. It is usually $1 or less and has little to no bearing on the stock's market price. Most individual investors in common stocks probably don't even realize there is a par value at all.

The par value of preferred shares, however, does matter. The most common par value of preferred stock is $100 per share, and they typically have long maturities, like 30 years or longer. They sometimes have no maturity date at all, meaning they are perpetual in nature.

Preferred shares have a priority claim versus common shares over dividends or asset distributions. This means that if a company went bankrupt and was liquidated, the preferred shareholders would get paid before the holders of common stock.

However, in exchange for the preferential treatment, preferred shareholders usually give up the right to any of the corporation's earnings that are in excess of their stated dividends. This limits the potential for price appreciation.

Here's an example:

A corporation issues preferred stock with a par value of $100 and a stated annual dividend of $8 per share. The owners of these preferred shares must receive the $8 per share dividend each year *before* the common stockholders can receive a penny in dividends.

The catch is, the preferred shareholders will get no more than the $8 dividend, even if the corporation's net income increases tenfold.

From an asset allocation perspective, preferred shares act more like bonds with their fixed dividend and limited potential for price appreciation. The payout might be more consistent and dependable than shares of common stock, but in times of inflation, rising interest rates, or expanding corporate profits, preferred shares can potentially fall in value or underperform other asset classes.

Like bonds, preferred shares do not confer any voting rights.

Most companies do *not* issue preferred shares. The entire preferred shares market in the U.S. is only about $350bn dollars. It is tiny in comparison to the total market capitalization of U.S. common stocks at over $48trn dollars!

Preferred shares can certainly be worth consideration, especially for income-focused investors, but most equity investors will be focused on common stocks.

It is common stock that gives investors the ability to fully capitalize on the long-term growth of successful companies.

———

Now we know what shares of stock are.

In the next chapter, we discuss how shares are owned and the different groups of investors who own them.

CHAPTER 5:
OWNING SHARES

TO PURCHASE A car, you can either go to a dealership, or in some cases you can go directly to the car company itself.

It is similar with stocks.

The most common way that stocks are purchased is through a brokerage firm, often just called a "broker."

A broker is a company that is authorized to buy and sell stocks. It is a middleman connecting buyers and sellers in all stocks.

From a user's perspective, it is like a dealership where you have the ability to purchase the stock of any company you want, and you have the ability to sell the stock of any company that you already own.

Brokerage accounts are accessible to most people and it's a relatively painless process to open one. Most will require basic personal information like your social security number, date of birth, and address.

Brokers are also required by regulators to ask certain questions pertaining to your type of employment, how you feel about taking financial risks, and other matters. It's not a quiz you need to prepare for; it's just the broker doing its due diligence in collecting information.

There are many different brokers who cater to different needs, so a little homework is recommended to find the best fit for your own circumstances. At the time of this writing, the four biggest brokerages in the U.S. based on customers and assets are Charles Schwab, Fidelity Investments, E*TRADE, and TD Ameritrade.

In Chapter 12 we describe specifically how to buy and sell stocks through common broker platforms.

While most buying and selling of stocks takes place through a broker, it is not the only option.

In some cases, you can bypass the dealership and purchase shares directly from the company you'd like to invest in. This approach is far less common and is not available for all companies.

FORMS OF OWNERSHIP

When you purchase a car, you take possession of it. The car sits in your driveway, and you have a paper title declaring that it's yours.

But how do you take possession of a stock?

There are three ways an investor can hold stock: a physical certificate, in street name registration, or in direct registration.

Back in the day, an investor would receive an actual paper certificate declaring their ownership. Believe it or not, it is still possible to take ownership in that way.

When you purchase a stock, be it through a broker or from the company itself, you can request to have the actual paper certificate sent to you. However, this service usually comes with a fee, and it places the burden of safekeeping the paper document on the owner, so it's becoming an outdated way of owning stocks. Many companies no longer offer paper certificates.

If you are an individual investor, the most likely way you will hold stocks is in **street name**. This means you hold the shares through a brokerage account, and while you are registered as the beneficial owner of the shares, it is the brokerage's name that is registered with the company.

So, if you were to buy shares of Chipotle (CMG) stock through a broker like TD Ameritrade, for example,

Chipotle doesn't know that you personally own its stock. Chipotle sees that TD Ameritrade owns a certain number of its shares, and TD Ameritrade keeps its own records as to which individuals are the owners.

Owning shares in street name is an accepted practice and helps facilitate the cheap and quick transfer of securities. It is the form in which the majority of shares are held.

One risk to owning stocks in street name, however, is if the broker with whom the shares are held were to misuse customer funds.

It is rare, but it has happened and could happen again, so it is a risk that investors should be aware of.

In the event that a brokerage company experiences its own financial troubles and needs to close its business, customer accounts are supposed to be kept separate and transferred to another company. But companies are run by people, and when times get desperate, there is always the possibility that they'll do something unethical in an attempt to save themselves.

If a broker either steals or loses a customer's investments, the customer is at least partially covered by insurance. Almost all legitimate broker-dealers in the United States are members of the **Securities Investor Protection Corporation** (**SIPC**), which partially protects investors in the event of misconduct. Investors holding securities in street name are covered by up to $500,000 of SIPC insurance.

For large investors or for those concerned with street name ownership, a third option for holding shares is through direct **registration**.

Not all companies offer direct registration, but for those that do, an investor can choose to be registered directly on the company's books as an owner of the stock.

The company won't send the investor a paper certificate, but they will (either directly or through a third-party transfer agent) send a statement of ownership, along with periodic account statements, dividends, annual reports, proxies, and other mailings.

One drawback of owning shares through direct registration is that it is less practical than keeping shares with a brokerage firm. With direct registration, an investor needs to have a transfer agent route buy and sell orders through a broker. It is a more time-consuming process than trading directly through a broker.

Personal story: the MF global collapse

It was Halloween 2011. I was trading natural gas futures through my broker, MF Global.

MF Global was a reputable firm with a 200-year history and business operations all over the world.

I sat at the computer, stressing over a risky trade when I heard on the television, "MF Global declares bankruptcy."

I got nervous, but I reassured myself: the customer accounts are separate from the company's own reckless trades, so I should be fine.

Then the next headline broke, "Shortfall in segregated client funds suspected."

Moments later, my account, the money in it, and my open trades were all frozen.

I panicked. I grabbed the phone and called the company.

"There's nothing we can do right now," the account representative explained to me, "we have to wait and find out more."

Unlike stock accounts, futures accounts do not carry SIPC insurance, but it has always been strict industry practice that client money remains segregated from company money.

Not in this case.

A few days later, MF Global's CEO, Jon Corzine, resigned with no replacement named. $600m in client funds was missing.

My open positions were transferred to a new broker, but with only a fraction of the collateral to back them up. I cut the positions and took the losses. At least I could sleep again knowing the trades were closed.

After several months of a trustee working through the customer claims, my account cash balance was eventually made whole. Luckily, what was a very stressful period ended with only minimal financial losses.

The lesson I took away from the experience was that, even though some degree of risk is inevitable, it is important to be cognizant of who you are doing business with and what degree of protection you have in a worst-case scenario.

The unthinkable happens, and protections like SIPC insurance for stocks and FIDC insurance for savings accounts should not be taken for granted.

COMMUNICATIONS

Regardless of the form in which you own stock, as a shareholder you will receive certain communications from the company either directly or through your broker.

The most common communications you will receive are annual reports and proxy statements.

The **annual report** is a state-of-the-company update. As the name suggests, the annual report is sent to shareholders once per year following the end of the company's fiscal year. The report is also made publicly available on the company's website.

The annual report usually includes an opening letter from the CEO, along with an update on business operations, financial performance, new product plans, and so on.

The investment community will often speak of the **Form 10-K**, which is similar to the annual report but usually includes more detailed financial statements. Companies are required to file a Form 10-K with the SEC within the 60-day period following the end of the company's fiscal year.

Side note: fiscal versus calendar years

Not all companies start their business year on January 1 and end it on Dec 31. Some do, but some don't—each company can choose the cadence of its fiscal year.

A company's fiscal year is a twelve-month period, like a normal year, but a company can choose the month on which it begins.

Companies usually end their fiscal years at the end of a calendar quarter—either the end of March, June, September, or December.

A fiscal year is denoted by the year in which the final month falls. For example, if a company's fiscal year runs from October 1, 2021 through September 30, 2022, that whole period marks their Fiscal 2022 year.

The company would then begin its fiscal 2023 year on October 1, 2022.

Companies with seasonal businesses often have fiscal years that differ from the calendar year. For instance, a retailer that does the majority of its sales during the holiday season may not want to end its business year on December 31. They are only a few days removed from the holiday madness, and it would be difficult to produce an annual report and the other required year-end statements at that time.

Investors will analyze a company's 10-K, as well as the **Form 10-Qs**, which are quarterly financial updates. While 10-Ks are submitted once at the end of the year and include audited financial statements, 10-Qs are due at the end of each of the first three quarters and include unaudited financial statements.

The 10-Qs provide timely updates to help investors track a company's progress through the year. It is like receiving periodic progress reports in school before the final report card arrives at the end of the semester.

The other main type of company communication shareholders receive is **proxy statements**.

The SEC requires companies to provide pertinent information to shareholders so they can make informed decisions about matters that will be brought up at an annual or special stockholder meeting. This type of information might include proposals for new additions to the board of directors, changes to executives' and directors' compensation, and other important business matters.

No matter how small a shareholder is, their vote counts and they have a right to know what they're voting on. Shareholders will receive these communications regardless of whether they own one share or one thousand shares.

I would note that if you own a non-voting class of shares, you may or may not receive such communications depending on the company, the exchange on which the stock is listed, and the nature of the notice.

I was an owner of Twitter (TWTR) shares (with voting rights) in 2022 when the company received a widely publicized takeover bid from Tesla founder Elon Musk. As a shareholder, I was entitled to vote on the adoption of the merger agreement.

I received through my brokerage account a 262-page proxy statement from Twitter detailing information about the upcoming vote.

The statement began with a two-page letter to shareholders signed by Twitter's CEO and board chair. In it they summarized what was at stake in the upcoming vote, and gave their recommendation on how shareholders should cast their votes.

Of course, investors are free to vote as they choose. They are also not required to cast a vote at all.

If you hold your shares in street name with a broker and you do not participate in a vote, the broker may in "routine matters" vote on your behalf at their discretion. Routine matters include things like the appointment of auditors and other actions that will not affect the privileges and rights associated with ownership of stock in the business.

In the case of a merger agreement, as with Twitter and Elon Musk, it is not a routine matter, so the broker cannot vote for you.

Most individual investors do not participate in corporate votes. According to data collected in 2021, only one-third of shares held by individual investors were represented by votes cast regarding corporate matters, compared with over 90% of institutionally owned shares.

RETAIL VERSUS INSTITUTIONAL OWNERSHIP

Retail investors are individuals. They are non-professionals who buy and sell stocks in their own personal accounts.

Retail investor is an umbrella term that includes the whole gamut of individual investors and their disparate aims. The 22-year-old buying GameStop (GME) shares on an internet trade tip is a retail investor. But so is the 60-year-old marketing executive with $2m invested in an S&P 500 index fund.

Financial media loves to gauge the sentiment of retail investors and deride them for their poor timing—buying stocks at highs and selling them at lows. Although, data suggests the pros aren't exactly Nostradamus-like in their market timing either.

The professionals are called **institutional investors**. Institutional investors are companies or organizations that invest money on behalf of other people, such as mutual funds, hedge funds, pension funds, and insurance companies. They get paid to invest.

Institutional investors manage pools of money, so they are the big fish in the pond. Over 70% of total shares of stock in the U.S. are owned by institutional investors.

They buy and sell bigger blocks of stock than retail investors, so their actions have a more meaningful impact on the direction of the market.

If you as an individual buy a few shares of Spotify (SPOT), you amount to a drop in the bucket and your order won't have a meaningful impact on the price of the stock. However, if a big institutional money manager decides to purchase millions of Spotify shares, they could prop up the stock or drive it higher in price.

It's not surprising that institutional investors are more active in shareholder votes than retail investors.

Small retail investors recognize that they don't have much voting power, and for the most part, they are only concerned about the price of their stock and the dividend payments that get deposited into their accounts.

Institutional investors, on the other hand, do have the power to influence corporate decisions. And their clients, whose money they are investing, expect them to do everything in their power to generate returns.

There is one type of institutional investor, known as an **activist investor**, that makes corporate action a direct part of its investment strategy.

An activist investor might aim to identify a company that has been underperforming its peers for no good reason other than complacency from the company's board and management team. It will then take a stake in the underperforming company and work to replace the board and management team with new people who are more aligned with its vision.

Perhaps the company is wasting money—employing too many people and flying around on corporate jets—and they need a kick in the butt to cut costs. Or maybe the CEO who's been running the show is just not getting the job done and should be replaced with someone more competent. In any case, these types of forced change can have meaningful effects on companies and their share prices.

Example: an activist investor

An activist investor that has gained some attention in recent years is Mantle Ridge, run by Paul Hilal.

Previously, while working at the well-known hedge fund Pershing Square, Mr. Hilal helped lead the firm's investment in Canadian Pacific Railroad (CP). At the time, in 2011, Canadian Pacific's operating margins were lower than its peers', but there was no clear structural reason why that should be the case.

Pershing Square acquired a large position in the stock, then gained enough support among shareholders to influence corporate decisions, and then installed a legendary railroad operator named Hunter Harrison as CEO. The idea was that under Hunter Harrison's management and expertise, the railroad would become more profitable, and the stock price would appreciate in response.

That's exactly what happened. The operating margin expanded, and the stock soared 150% in five years. Pershing Square made over $2.5bn in profit.

Shortly after the successful CP investment, Mr. Hilal left Pershing Square to start his own hedge fund called Mantle Ridge. The initial goal was to replicate what he had done with Canadian Pacific with another railroad company, CSX.

Similar to Canadian Pacific, the CSX railroad had profit margins that were lower than those of its peers, so the thought was: Hunter Harrison can probably fix things here, too.

So, in late 2016 Mantle Ridge began accumulating a position in CSX stock. In early 2017, to avoid getting into a proxy battle (which is an unfriendly contest for control over an organization), CSX agreed to Mantle Ridge's request to install Hunter Harrison as CEO.

Unfortunately, Mr. Harrison passed away unexpectedly in December 2017. He didn't get to personally oversee all the operational changes he had planned for the railroad, but the team he helped assemble did.

Mantle Ridge made out fine on its investment. They sold most of their CSX shares in 2019, roughly doubling their money in less than three years.

Not all institutional investors are activists. Activist investors control only a small subset of professionally managed money.

INSTITUTIONAL INVESTMENT APPROACHES

There are many different styles and objectives within the institutional equity investor bucket. The simplest way conceptually to split the bucket is into two broad groups: long-onlys and hedge funds.

Long-onlys are fund managers that only go "long" stocks. Going long means that they buy stocks for the purpose of investment.

An *investor* has a longer-term mindset. They take a financial stake in what they believe is a good or undervalued business, and they trust that over time the company's performance will result in a profit for them as shareholders.

This is different from *trading*. A trader typically has a shorter-term mindset and is betting on the near-term directional move of a stock. It may or may not have anything to do with an opinion on the company's long-term prospects.

Long-only funds include what most people think of as normal investment firms. They purchase stocks that they think are good investments, and they sell those stocks when they no longer think they are good investments. They aim to hold positions for years and do not speculate on short-term price movements.

Mutual funds are an example of a long-only fund. A portfolio manager and a team of analysts select stocks based on their own criteria, and they aim to manage a portfolio that will outperform the market.

The people who invest their money with a mutual fund pay a fee for the service because they believe the excess returns generated by the professional stock selection process will exceed the returns from simply investing in a fund that tracks a broader market index. We discuss indexes in Chapter 12.

For this reason, the performance of a long-only mutual fund is judged against a benchmark rather than in absolute terms. Since stocks for the most part move in tandem with the overall market, clients would not expect their long-only stock fund to show a positive return in a year where the whole market was down 20%.

They might instead hope to see that even though the market-tracking index was down 20%, their actively managed fund was only down 15%. And on the flip side, in a year where the market was up 20%, they would hope to see their actively managed mutual fund up more than that.

Hedge funds, on the other hand, are meant to be what the name implies—a hedge.

A hedge is an investment intended to offset potential losses or gains that may be incurred by another investment.

You may have heard the phrase "hedge your bet." It means to do something that will prevent total failure if events don't unfold as you planned.

For example, if you have a significant portion of your wealth invested in stocks and other correlated assets, your net worth will take a major hit in a big down year in the market. By allocating some money to a hedge fund, the idea is that some of your wealth will be invested in a way that is uncorrelated to the rest of your long-only investments. The hope is that the hedge fund investment could make money in years where the rest of your portfolio loses money.

One way hedge funds can achieve uncorrelated returns is by betting on the price of a stock to go down, which is called **short selling**.

When a money manager shorts a stock, it borrows shares of stock from a broker and sells them in the market. They are betting that the price of the shares will decline, at which point they can buy back the shares at a lower price, then return them to the broker, making a profit in the process.

Think of it this way: every trade or investment at some point must have a buy and a sell. Whether the duration of the trade is ten minutes or ten years, the hope is always that the purchase price is lower than the sale price. That same logic applies to shorting stock, only the order of the trades is reversed.

If you buy a stock at $50 per share and sell it at $100 per share, you made $50 per share in profit. The order in which the buy and sell took place does not matter.

Shorting stocks is only one of many alternative strategies deployed by hedge funds. They can also trade options, futures, credit default swaps, and a whole host of other creative strategies. It is all in an effort to generate uncorrelated returns.

Short selling: an analogy

Imagine your friend just bought a sweater for $100 at a department store.

With Christmas just a few weeks away, you are convinced that the store will soon offer a discount on the sweater, at which point it could be purchased much cheaper.

To profit on your idea, you say to your friend, "Hey, can I borrow your sweater for a few weeks and then return it back to you? I'll buy you a candy bar as payment for letting me borrow it."

Your friend agrees, so you give him the candy bar, you take the sweater and return it to the store for $100. You put the $100 in your pocket, then you wait.

Sure enough, a couple weeks later the store offers a 50% store-wide discount, and you walk in and purchase the sweater for $50.

You give the sweater back to your friend, but you now have an extra $50 in your pocket! You just profited from your prediction that the sweater would fall in price.

That is the idea behind short selling. It is a challenging and risky endeavor that even most professionals struggle with.

Ironically, some equity hedge funds have given up on shorting stocks since it has proven so hard to do. There is technically now a bucket of long-only hedge funds known as **long-only absolute return funds**.

Like traditional hedge funds, long-only absolute return funds aim to generate positive absolute returns regardless of how the broader market performs. They sometimes make concentrated bets on stocks they believe are undervalued or misunderstood by the market. They may also look to hedge risk through the use of options or other derivatives.

A derivative is a financial contract whose value is dependent on an underlying asset such as a stock or a commodity. In chapter 14 we will discuss two of the most commonly traded derivatives—options and futures.

No discussion of institutional investing would be complete without mentioning the massive growth in **quantitative investing**.

There is not always a pondering human at the other end of your stock trade. A lot of actively managed funds are now driven by statistical models and algorithms that remove the emotional pitfalls of investing from the equation.

In fact, the best performing hedge fund of all time, Renaissance Technologies, was and is a quantitative investing (quant) fund.

The fund, founded by PhD mathematician James Simon, applied complex mathematical pattern recognition to trading. Since 1988, Renaissance's signature fund has generated average annual returns over 60% and has earned total profits in excess of $100bn. James Simon's personal net worth is estimated to be over $20bn.

So, according to the numbers, the best investor of all time is a quant.

However, more and more dollars are being allocated to quantitative investing strategies, so with more competition on the field, exceptional returns could be harder to come by.

We'll see if a human can ever catch the machine. Only time will tell.

History lesson: the birth of hedge funds

The first hedge fund is said to have been started in 1949 by Alfred Winslow Jones. As he saw it, there were two main risks to stock investing: market risk and stock-specific risk.

His simple but groundbreaking idea was to create a market-neutral portfolio, where he would be long stocks that he thought would outperform versus short stocks he thought would underperform.

By having both long and short positions open at the same time, he would cancel out the directional moves of the broader market and be left with pure stock-picking alpha.

Alpha, which is the goal of all investors and traders, is excess return relative to the market or some other benchmark. It is proof of stock-picking skill.

In 1952 he added an incentive fee and converted his fund to a limited partnership. This was the first product available to investors combining a hedged strategy with the use of leverage (i.e. borrowed money) and a 20% performance fee.

By the 1960s, interest in hedge funds began to take off. A 1966 article in *Fortune* magazine created some buzz by highlighting the outperformance of Jones's investment vehicle. The article claimed that Jones had outperformed the best mutual fund over the prior five years by 44%, even accounting for the high fees.

Within the next few years, many new hedge funds were established, including the legendary George Soros's Quantum Fund.

Now we understand how shares are held and who they are held by.

In the next chapter, we discuss how investors make money in stocks—dividends and capital gains.

CHAPTER 6: DIVIDENDS AND CAPITAL GAINS

A S OWNERS OF common stock, we want to capitalize on a company's growth.

But how does owning a stock translate into actual dollars in your bank account?

There are two ways that investors in common stock can make a profit: dividends and capital gains.

DIVIDENDS

When I sign in to my brokerage account, the value of my portfolio may have increased for either of two reasons: the prices of my stocks went up, or I received a dividend payment.

Higher stock prices are great, but they might be temporary. Only time will tell.

The dividend payment, however, is permanent. It is cash deposited in my account. I can do whatever I want with it.

A **dividend** is a distribution of a company's earnings to its shareholders.

When a company generates cash from its operations, it must choose what to do with it. The decision to pay out that cash in the form of a dividend is made by the company's board of directors. The board is responsible for deciding if a dividend will be paid at all, and if so, for how much.

In the United States, dividends are often paid quarterly and in cash. There are some cases where dividends are paid out in the form of additional stock, but typically, when investors talk about dividends, they are talking about cash distributions.

The best dividend stocks tend to be issued by big, well-established companies with predictable profits.

A small company that is growing rapidly will probably want to reinvest the cash in its business. They need to devote that precious cash into hiring workers, funding research and development, and marketing to increase brand awareness and expand their market share. The dividend payments will have to wait, and their investors will likely understand that.

On the other hand, a mature company whose growth has slowed but who generates a lot of profit, will probably want to reward its owners with periodic dividend payments.

These mature companies still need to reinvest in their own businesses to sustain their competitive positions, but they don't need to reinvest all their cash. They have an excess, and investors in these flush companies will likely expect some of the excess to be doled out in periodic cash payments.

Dividends are often cited as a percentage relative to the share price, known as the **dividend yield**.

For example, if a company pays a dividend of $3 per share, and the stock is trading at $100 per share, then the dividend yield is 3%.

This means that for every $100 invested in the company, you could expect to receive $3 back each year in the form of cash dividend payments. Usually, the $3 per share annual dividend payment would be divided into four quarterly payments.

A high dividend yield can be attractive to investors, but unfortunately investing is not quite as simple as just buying the highest yield. What seems too good to be true often is.

If a company has what appears to be an extraordinarily high dividend yield compared to its peers, it could be an indication that it is unsustainable. The yield may be high because investors are selling the stock in anticipation of a dividend cut.

A company is not obligated to maintain its dividend. If business conditions worsen or the company's board feels there is a better use for the cash, the company can reduce the dividend or even eliminate it entirely.

One way to gauge the sustainability of the dividend is to look at the **dividend payout ratio**.

The dividend payout ratio is calculated by dividing the yearly dividend per share by the yearly earnings per share (EPS).

For example, if a company were to pay $1 in total dividends per share in a given year, and they generated $2 in total earnings per share (EPS) in that same year, then their dividend payout ratio would be 50% ($1 ÷ $2 = 0.5, or 50%).

This simple ratio indicates the percentage of a company's total earnings that are being paid out in dividends. In this case, for every $1 of profit generated, the company paid out 50 cents in dividends.

If a company is covering its dividend payment with only a small fraction of its total earnings, it could be inferred that the dividend payment is likely safe.

However, if a company is having to devote the majority of its earnings to make the dividend payments, it becomes more likely that any unfortunate hiccup in the business could put the dividend payment at risk.

A general rule of thumb is that a dividend payout ratio under 50% is considered stable, while over 50% could start to become worrisome.

Case Study: cutting the dividend

The General Motors Company (GM) is an iconic American car company that was founded in 1908. GM paid reliable, consistent dividends for several decades, including a 50c dividend each quarter from 1997 to 2005.

When General Motor's business began to falter in the mid-2000s, the share price fell from over $60 in early 2003 to under $20 in early 2006, and the dividend yield topped 10%.

For many investors, a 10% yield from a company with an esteemed history seemed too good to be true.

It was.

In February 2006, GM cut its dividend in half to 25c per share. And then in May 2008, the company suspended its dividend altogether. Just a year later, in 2009, GM declared bankruptcy and the stock price went to zero.

General Motors ended up being bailed out by the U.S. government during the financial crisis, and the stock later went public again in October 2011, but the pain for investors had already been felt. Owners of GM stock prior to the bankruptcy lost their entire investment.

When a company announces that it will pay a dividend, there are a few noteworthy dates for investors to pay attention to.

The **announcement date**, or **declaration date**, is when the company first announces publicly to its shareholders that it plans to pay a dividend.

The **payment date** is the date on which the dividend payment will actually be made. This is the date when the cash will be sent out and deposited in shareholders' accounts.

Since shares of the stock are being bought and sold by new people every minute of every day, it raises the question: who gets the dividend payment?

That is determined by the **record date**. The record date is the cutoff date—a date picked by the company to determine which shareholders are eligible to receive the dividend. Owners of the stock on the record date will receive the next dividend payment.

What's important for investors to note is that when a stock is purchased, the official ownership of the stock does not transfer immediately. In the United States, it currently takes two business days for a trade to settle. This is known as the **T+2** system.

So, in order to qualify for the dividend payment by being an owner of the stock on the record date, you would need to purchase the stock two business days *before* the record date.

The day immediately prior to the record date is known as the **ex-dividend date** because it is the date on which it would be too late to purchase the stock and receive the next dividend payment.

Here's a real example of this:

On July 30, 2020, Apple (AAPL) declared that it would pay a quarterly dividend of $0.82 per share on August 13. The payment would go to all shareholders of record as of Monday, August 10.

Since it takes two business days for ownership to transfer (for a new owner of the stock to show up in the record), it means that you would have to purchase the stock on or before Thursday, August 6 to qualify for the dividend.

That day in between—Friday, August 7—was the ex-dividend date because it was on that day that new buyers of AAPL would no longer qualify for the upcoming dividend payment.

When a stock goes ex-dividend, the share price typically drops by the amount of the dividend paid to reflect the fact that new shareholders are not entitled to that payment.

As a knowledgeable investor, these dates are good to be aware of, but are not often something you need to focus on. If you are investing in a company for the long term, it probably won't matter too much to you whether or not you receive the next quarterly dividend payment.

A quarterly dividend is like an allowance. It is a small, regular payment the shareholder gets each quarter for being an owner of the business.

Sometimes, however, the shareholder gets a surprise bonus! A **special dividend** is when a company decides to make a one-time dividend payment to its shareholders. Typically, a special dividend will be of an amount greater than the normal quarterly dividends.

Similar to when a company has a good year and pays a bonus to its employees, a company's board might decide to pay a special dividend to its shareholders when the company has been doing well and finds itself with a surplus of cash.

An example of a company that has paid multiple special dividends is Costco Wholesale Corporation (COST). Costco is a membership-only retailer based in the United States, which has been an elite performer in terms of generating consistently strong sales and earnings.

In November 2020, Costco was paying a regular dividend of $0.70 per quarter. However, since the company was performing so well and had excess cash, it announced that it would pay a special dividend in December of 2020 of $10 per share, equating to a dividend yield of 2.63%.

That special dividend was the fourth that Costco had paid within eight years. They had previously paid a $7 special dividend in 2017, $5 in 2015, and $7 in 2012.

If you were an owner of COST stock, you were likely happy to receive the bonus cash payout.

REINVESTING DIVIDENDS

When a dividend is paid, the cash is deposited in the investor's account. The investor is then free to do with the cash as they please.

One option is to reinvest the dividends back into shares of the stock. By consistently using the quarterly dividends to purchase more stock, earnings from the investment can compound over time, potentially leading to greater returns.

The concept of **compounding** is paramount in investing.

Albert Einstein is quoted as saying, "Compound interest is the eighth wonder of the world. He who understands it, earns it; he who doesn't, pays it."

By consistently using dividend payments to purchase more shares of stock, you increase the base on which the dividends are paid.

For example, if you own $100 of stock that pays a 5% annual dividend, at the end of one year you will have $105. If you reinvest the $5 in more shares, the following year you will earn 5% of $105, or $5.25. The next year, 5% of $110.25, which is $5.51. And so on.

Over short periods of time the numbers seem underwhelming, but the magic of compounding is what happens over long periods of time.

Over 50 years of reinvesting dividends, that initial $100 in a 5% yielding stock would become worth $1,146.74.

Imagine that concept applied to the entirety of a person's savings over the course of their whole lifetime. After 40 to 50 years of working and saving, they could have many multiples more saved for retirement if they allowed their savings to compound than if they did not.

Reinvesting dividends can be accomplished manually. You can take the cash received from the dividend payment and use it to submit a new buy order for additional shares.

The issue you might run into is that the dividend payment you receive is smaller than the cost of one share. For example, if you receive $30 in dividends and the price of one share is $60, you won't have enough cash to purchase an additional share.

Some brokerages are now offering the ability to purchase **fractional shares**—meaning, you can purchase less than one full share. If you have this option, then you could reinvest your $30 dividend by purchasing ½ of a $60 share.

Investors should be aware that commission fees can eat away the economics of dividend reinvestment. For instance, if you receive a dividend payment for $14 and your brokerage charges a $7 fee per trade, you would be spending 50% of your dividend payment on the trade. That is not a formula for making money.

One way to alleviate this issue is to enroll in a **Dividend Reinvestment Plan** (**DRIP**). A DRIP is a program offered by some companies that allows investors to reinvest their cash dividends into additional shares or fractional shares of the company's stock.

With a DRIP, the new shares are purchased directly from the company on the date of the dividend payment. Most DRIPs allow investors to buy shares commission-free or for a small fee. Some DRIPS even allow investors to purchase shares at a discount to the current market price.

Not all companies pay dividends, and not all companies that do pay dividends offer DRIPs.

A good place to look for DRIPs is with a group of companies known as the Dividend Aristocrats. These are big, well-established companies that meet certain size and liquidity requirements and have a 25+ year history of making dividend increases. The list of Dividend Aristocrats includes many well-known, powerhouse corporations, such as Caterpillar, ExxonMobil, McDonald's, and PepsiCo.

Income received from dividends is taxable. In the United States, ordinary dividends are taxed at an individual's ordinary income tax rate. However, most dividends from common stocks bought on U.S. exchanges are distinguished as **qualified dividends**.

Qualified dividends are taxable federally at the capital gains rate, which depends on the investor's income but is often lower than the individual's ordinary income tax rate.

It should be noted that the Internal Review Service (IRS) requires investors to hold shares for a minimum period of time to benefit from the lower tax rate on qualified dividends.

The time frame is rather specific. The current rule is that common stock investors must hold the shares for more than 60 days during the 121-day period that starts 60 days before the ex-dividend date.

The simple way I think of it is that if I've held the stock for at least a few months, I'll likely get the qualified rate.

One way that investors can potentially lessen the impact of taxes is by holding dividend-paying stocks in tax-advantaged retirement accounts like 401(k)s. These accounts do not require the payment of taxes on dividends until the holder begins drawing down money from the funds. This can allow the investment to compound at a higher rate since the full amount of dividend payments (not the after-tax amount) gets reinvested in the underlying stock.

CAPITAL GAINS

Not all companies pay dividends, but that doesn't mean you can't make money owning their stocks.

The other way that an investor can make money by owning a stock is if the share price increases.

This, of course, is part of the allure of stocks—that you could purchase an asset that has the potential to significantly appreciate in value.

But it's a two-sided coin. Share prices can go up, but they can also go down. When an investor purchases a stock, its value will fluctuate day to day, sometimes significantly.

When an investor officially locks in profit by selling the stock for a higher price than she bought it, it is known as a **capital gain**.

A FOCUS ON SHARE PRICE APPRECIATION

An investor should recognize that not all companies think about dividends versus capital gains in the same way.

Depending on where a company is in its lifecycle, it may explicitly focus on increasing its share price rather than paying dividends.

Mature companies that are generating profit may view dividend payments as an appropriate allocation of cash. It makes sense for them. After years of solidifying their place in the world, these companies have achieved a high degree of success and can now spread the wealth. Of all the seeds scattered on the ground, they are the select few that became mature trees, and they now yield fruit.

But for younger or less-established companies, paying dividends is not always considered the most productive use of cash. They are saplings trying to claim their place in the forest. Those who don't reach the canopy quick enough get crowded out and will never see daylight. The fruit will have to wait.

For these growing companies it makes more sense to invest cash back into the business to fuel continued growth.

For investors, collecting regular dividend payments is nice, but if you bet on a sapling that turns into a mature tree, your shares will likely undergo a significant appreciation in price.

Why?

Because ultimately, a company's current value—its stock price—is dependent on the outlook for its future earnings.

If a company is making a nice dividend payment but its business is losing ground to competitors, that's a problem. The mature tree is dropping apples, but the trunk is rotting, so it's clear that there won't be many apples to go around in the future.

That bleak outlook for future earnings will likely result in a declining stock price.

On the other hand, a company might not be paying any dividends now, but it is consistently growing sales, improving its profitability, and gaining market share in its respective industry. In this case, there's no apples being distributed yet, but investors will feel confident that there are many to come.

That optimistic outlook for future earnings will likely drive the stock price higher.

SHARE REPURCHASES

Over time, companies need to strike a balance between investing in growth and returning cash to shareholders.

Returning cash to shareholders, however, does not only need to come in the form of dividend payments. An indirect way that companies can return cash to shareholders is by repurchasing their own stock.

When a company uses cash to repurchase its own stock it is known as **share repurchases** or **buybacks**.

When a company repurchases its own stock, the shares are removed from the market—meaning, there are fewer shares available.

If the company's earnings remain the same but get divided between fewer shares, the earnings per share increases. This theoretically makes each share more valuable.

For example, if a company makes $100 and there are 100 shares outstanding, each share of stock would entitle its owner to $1 of profit. But if the company bought back and retired half of its shares, that same $100 of earnings gets divided between only 50 shares, entitling the holder of each share to $2.

All else equal, you would pay more for the share entitling you to $2 of earnings versus the share entitling you to $1 earnings, so the price of the stock should increase.

Share repurchases have surged in recent decades. There are strong opinions on both sides as to whether that's a good thing or a bad thing.

Those in favor of using cash to repurchase shares will point to the tax benefits and financial flexibility it offers relative to dividends.

Public companies are usually **C corporations** (**C-corps**). With this corporate structure, the company is taxed as a separate entity from its owners. So when a public company pays a dividend to its shareholders, it gets double taxed. It is first taxed at the corporate level, and then it is taxed again at the individual level.

By using company cash to directly repurchase shares, a buyback program is a way to return value to shareholders without creating a taxable event in the form of a dividend payment.

Companies will also tout that share repurchases give them more flexibility than committing to a dividend. Dividends are like an allowance paid to children. They come to be expected and there's a revolt if one is missed!

Companies would sometimes rather not commit to the regular payments. They'd prefer to be *opportunistic*, and if they have the cash to repurchase shares at what they feel is an attractive price, then they'll do it.

Those opposed to share repurchases would say there are two problematic questions regarding opportunistic buybacks: whose opportunity is it, and what's an opportunistic price?

A lot of senior executives are compensated in some way based on their company's share price. There could be a personal incentive for them to temporarily juice the stock price higher instead of paying out dividends.

This could lead to shortsightedness—doing what's good for the stock price in the near-term, but not necessarily what's best for the business or its long-term investors.

Additionally, individual investors are notorious for being poor timers of the market. They buy stocks at highs and sell stocks at lows. Companies are run by individuals, and therefore aren't great at timing stock purchases either.

When times are good, companies can pile money into buying back overpriced shares only to see them crater when times turn tough.

The American discount retailer Big Lots (BIG) saw two years of declining earnings and a falling stock price leading up to the Covid-19 pandemic. The stock was trading for $25 per share in February 2020 prior to the pandemic-led market crash.

In the following year, Big Lots benefited greatly from the Covid-19 environment as people stayed home and spent stimulus money on things Big Lots sold, like food, furniture, and electronics. The stock price soared as a result, and management used cash to *opportunistically* buy back stock at $60 per share.

A year later, Covid concerns abated, peoples' spending habits normalized, and shares of Big Lots fell back below $25 per share (as Figure 1 shows).

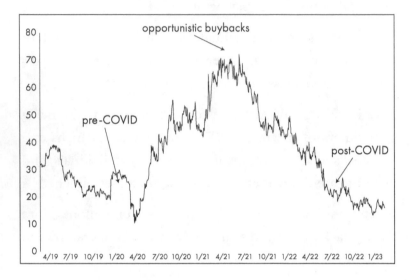

FIGURE 1: BIG LOTS (BIG)—4YR

Source: FactSet data and analytics

THE PERFORMANCE OF CAPITAL GAINS VERSUS DIVIDENDS

Times always change, but over the past couple decades the general trend in the U.S. has been that companies and investors have prioritized capital gains over dividend payments.

Especially coming out of the 2008 Financial Crisis, capital gains outshone dividends as low interest rates and technological disruption led to big gains in some new-age growth companies. These disruptive companies saw their market capitalizations expand exponentially as their businesses came to dominate their respective markets.

Going back to 1930, capital gains have accounted for around 60% of the S&P 500's historical total return, while dividends accounted for around 40%. But in the 2010s the scale was significantly tilted, with capital gains accounting for 83% of the total return.

Historically, in decades in which the total return from the stock market was below 10%—as it was in the 1940s, 1960s, 1970s, and 2000s—dividends made a larger contribution to returns.

Dividends can sometimes come back into focus as earnings growth slows or stock prices fall. For example, dividends were de-emphasized in the 1990s as stock prices soared and exciting new companies prioritized funding their growth over dividend payments. However, when the dot-com bubble burst at the end of the decade, and both stock prices and business outlooks came back down to reality, investors once again cared about dividends.

A decade later, following the financial crisis in 2008–2009, an ultra-low interest rate policy by the Federal Reserve combined with extraordinary technological advancements fostered an investment environment where dividends were again de-prioritized in favor of growth.

The trend was interrupted in 2022 as rising inflation forced the Federal Reserve to raise interest rates, resulting in a steep decline in the share prices of many high-growth companies.

At the time of this writing, there is again renewed investor interest in dividends. Whether or not the change in sentiment back to dividends will persist will likely depend on several factors, including inflation, monetary policy, interest rates, economic growth, and technological developments.

Regardless of broad sentiment shifts on dividends versus capital gains, there are always opportunities to profit from strong individual companies.

If you buy a young sapling and sell it once it becomes a mature tree, you've made money on capital gains.

If you buy a mature tree and collect the fruit each year, you've made money on dividends.

If you're an astute, long-term investor, there's no reason you can't own the tree through the whole transformation.

———

Now we know the ways in which money can be made from stocks.

In the next chapter, we discuss how shares are valued by analysts and what causes share prices to move.

CHAPTER 7:
VALUING SHARES

Y OU TURN ON CNBC and hear the headline, "Morgan Stanley issues a buy rating on Home Depot (HD) with a $400 per share price target."

You may ask yourself, who is Morgan Stanley and how did they come up with a value of $400 per share for this company?

Morgan Stanley is one of many firms that provide research and recommendations on stock investments to professional investors.

Recommendations from research firms typically include a rating—like *buy*, *sell*, or *neutral*—and a price target. The price target is usually twelve months out, meaning it's the price per share they expect the stock to trade at a year from now.

Professional investors often monitor these firms' research closely, but when a notable firm makes a strong prediction on a stock, it sometimes also gets public attention on CNBC and other financial news outlets.

It is important to realize that price targets on Wall Street are very much moving targets. They change all the time and are often not reached.

There are many factors that could cause a stock's price to deviate drastically from analyst predictions. Investors should never blindly follow a buy or sell recommendation.

While valuation analyses may seem like the sophisticated work of professionals, the principles are intuitive and can help even novice investors gain a better understanding of the risk versus reward of a stock.

Ultimately, valuation is a subjective analysis. In practice, equity valuations are often similar to how you might assess the value of your home. You look at recent comparables, like what price your neighbor's house sold for last month, and then you think about the unique features of your house, like it being closer to the beach, having more square footage, or being recently remodeled.

With stocks too, the first thing people often look at is what the closest comparable stocks are selling for. That's why when the market is strong and stock prices are moving higher, analyst price targets tend to also move higher, and when the market is weak and stock prices are moving lower, analyst price targets tend to move lower too.

The tides of the ocean are usually more significant than individual waves.

That doesn't mean valuation analysis isn't useful.

Investing money in a stock requires confidence. In the short term, stock prices can blow around like leaves in the wind. It's hard to make any decisions based on that.

A good valuation analysis attempts to put a stick in the ground and make a reasonable assessment of where a stock's price should ultimately settle.

VALUATION TECHNIQUES

There are several standard approaches used by analysts to assess and predict the value of a stock.

In theory, the value of a share of stock today is the present value of all its future cash flows. That's the idea behind a standard valuation method called a **discounted cash flow analysis**.

If you knew how much cash a company would return to you over time, you could ballpark what that'd be worth to you today.

Keep in mind, all else equal, a dollar in your pocket today is more meaningful than a dollar in your pocket years from now. If someone asked whether you'd like them to give you $100 dollars now or $100 dollars ten years from now, you would likely take the $100 dollars now.

A discounted cash flow analysis will estimate the future cash flows of a business, and then discount them to account for the time value of money.

While the logic behind the process makes sense, the problem is that estimating the future cash flows of a business is guesswork. We humans are pretty poor predictors of anything, let alone the cash that a company will generate many years from now.

A simpler method for valuing a stock is to use a **price-to-earnings ratio**, also known as a **P/E ratio**. This is an approach used by many professional analysts on Wall Street.

The P/E ratio, sometimes referred to as P/E multiple, is simply the price of a company's share divided by the amount of earnings per share (EPS) the company generates.

For example, if Nike (NKE) shares are currently trading at $100 each, and the company earned $4 per share in earnings last year, then the stock's P/E ratio is 25.

This means that investors are paying $25 for every $1 of earnings.

The lower the P/E ratio, the cheaper the stock is considered to be.

Thinking about a stock in this way can be a useful comparison tool, especially when comparing it to similar companies.

If, for example, fellow athletics wear company Under Armour (UAA) is trading at a P/E ratio of 20, that means you could pay only $20 for every $1 of earnings.

Based on that, you may think Nike is too expensive relative to Under Armour. Or you may think Nike deserves to be more expensive than Under Armour because it has a stronger brand and better growth prospects. That's where subjective analysis still plays a role.

Professional analysts are often more concerned about what will happen than what already happened. For that reason, when they use P/E ratios they typically assess a stock's current price compared to the amount of earnings the company is expected to make in the year ahead rather than what it already made in the year behind. This is known as a forward P/E, as compared to a trailing P/E which uses last year's EPS.

The calculation for the forward P/E is the same as it was for the trailing P/E, only the EPS is a prediction for what the company will earn this year rather than what it actually earned last year.

Typically, the number used as the EPS prediction is the **consensus** estimate, which is the average estimate of all the professional analysts who cover the stock.

In the Nike example, if the shares are trading at $100 each, and consensus expects the company to make $5 per share this year, then the forward P/E ratio is 20.

As you can see, if a company is able to significantly increase its earnings, the P/E ratio comes down quickly, and the stock begins to look more cheaply valued.

This is why companies that are growing quickly tend to trade at high P/E ratios while companies that are growing slowly or not at all tend to trade at low P/E multiples.

To illustrate the concept, imagine that you are in your twenties and have the ability to invest in your friends—you can purchase a stake in them now that would entitle you to a percentage of their annual income for the rest of their lives.

One friend is highly driven, was valedictorian of an Ivy League school, and is already getting promotions and raises at a top-performing hedge fund. The other friend has no ambition, spends most of his time playing video games, and does odd jobs for cash.

It is of course possible that the latter friend ends up making more money—there is beauty in unconventional paths—but right now you would naturally pay a higher price (i.e., a higher P/E multiple) for the valedictorian's earnings.

If the valedictorian remains on track and keeps getting promotions, raises, and bonus payments, the premium paid now for a share of his earnings could end up looking insignificant with time.

The P/E ratio can be very useful, but it is not suitable for all companies. Some companies don't have any earnings at all. However, if they are young and growing, that doesn't mean their stocks are worthless.

In cases like this, stocks are sometimes valued based on sales.

The **price-to-sales ratio** (**P/S ratio**) is like the P/E ratio, but instead of earnings it shows how much investors are willing to pay per dollar of sales for a stock.

Again, the lower the P/S ratio, the cheaper the stock.

Similar to the P/E ratio, companies that are showing above-average growth are typically more expensive, which means they will trade at a higher P/S ratio than peers.

Sometimes, instead of valuing a stock based just on its share price, analysts will use **enterprise value**, abbreviated as EV.

The difference is that enterprise value takes into account a company's debt and cash. It is a closer approximation of what it would cost an acquiror to buy out a whole company.

An acquiror would be responsible for the debts of a company but would keep its cash, so the EV calculation takes the total value of shares (the company's market cap) but adds back debt and subtracts cash.

For this reason, it is sometimes thought that EV/Sales is a more accurate valuation metric than Price/Sales, since it considers the amount of debt the company will have to repay at some point.

The most common way that enterprise value is used as a valuation metric is in comparison to a company's EBITDA, or earnings before interest, taxes, depreciation, and amortization (i.e., the accounting practice of spreading the cost of an intangible asset over its useful life).

The ratio, known as **EV/EBITDA**, is more nuanced than the standard P/E ratio in that it compares the value of a company (including its debt) to the company's cash earnings, less its non-cash expenses.

It can sometimes be more useful than P/E in comparing firms with different degrees of debt, or with capital-intensive businesses with high levels of depreciation or amortization.

Like the P/E and P/S ratios, a stock with a low EV/EBITDA ratio is considered to be cheaper than a stock with a high EV/EBITDA ratio.

There are various other metrics that you may encounter that can be used to assess the value of a company, like book value, free cash flow, and so on. We won't go into all of them here.

Ultimately, valuation is just as much an art as it is a science. It is up to an investor to decide which valuation technique is most appropriate for a given stock, and it is up to the investor to subjectively assess the information.

GOING AGAINST THE GRAIN

Reviewing valuation metrics like the price-to-earnings ratio can give you a sense for how cheap or expensive a stock is, but keep in mind that it is a simple calculation that anyone can do. You are not unearthing any new information that market participants don't already know.

For that reason, when professionals on Wall Street make a strong buy or sell recommendation on a stock, it is usually because they have a non-consensus opinion on either the company's earnings estimates or the multiple, or both. In other words, they have a view on a stock that is different than what most people think.

In the hypothetical example of Nike (NKE), the stock was trading at $100 per share, which equated to a forward P/E multiple of 20x the average analyst EPS estimate of $5.

Those are the numbers that are reflected in the market right now. If you agree that the Nike is likely to make $5 in EPS, and you agree that Nike's business is worth a 20 multiple, then you agree the stock is currently worth $100 per share. You therefore don't have much of a call on the stock.

However, if you've done some kind of differentiated research on Nike and believe that the company will make much more money than most people expect, then you are making a call that the stock is undervalued and that it should be bought.

For example, perhaps your research on Nike's sales trends leads you to believe that it should generate $6 in EPS next year. And your research on Nike's competitive advantages versus its peers makes you believe the stock deserves a 25 multiple.

Then, in your assessment, the stock should trade up to $150 per share. If you are correct, that would end up being a 50% gain for those who took your advice and bought the stock now at $100.

Essentially, this is the aim of analysts and investors on Wall Street—to identify companies whose stocks are either underappreciated or overappreciated by the market.

It is a difficult endeavor because most information is publicly available and there are thousands of smart people assessing the same material. This leads to somewhat efficient markets where, for the most part, stocks trade at valuations relative to their peers that make sense.

Price is a moving target.

As discussed, stocks are valued based on *expected* earnings and a *subjective* multiple—both of which are moving targets.

That's why stock prices constantly move.

The expectations for a company's earnings can shift with every piece of news.

Are sales tracking ahead or behind plan? Are new competitors emerging? Are input costs rising or falling? Is the industry growing or shrinking?

Endless data points continuously affect investors' expectations for future earnings. As the data points emerge and expectations change, so will the stock price.

The multiple applied to those changing earnings expectations also fluctuates, many times for factors not even directly related to the company.

Are central banks raising or lowering interest rates? Is the economy accelerating or decelerating? Is geopolitical risk increasing or decreasing?

These types of things can determine how much investors are willing to pay for stocks in general, regardless of the company's expected earnings.

And if that's not enough, there is also plain old sentiment.

Ultimately, stocks are bought and sold by individuals, and they are free to buy or sell them based on any idea or emotion they want, even if it's irrational.

GameStop (GME) shares went from $1.20 to $120 (split adjusted) in just four months in 2020–2021 because the idea of buying the stock went viral on the internet. There was no change in the business or the economy to justify that type of price move, but people wanted to buy the stock anyway (as seen in Figure 2).

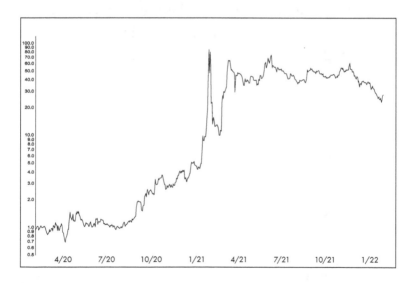

FIGURE 2: GAMESTOP (GME)—3YR

Source: FactSet data and analytics

Stock moves that are based purely on sentiment are often not sustained, but that doesn't make the moves any less real as they're happening.

The bottom line is: there are a lot of forces acting on a stock's price. At any point in time the price is a reflection of real results and probabilities, but also guesswork, opinion, and even emotion.

Prices will always fluctuate based on continuous shifts in these and other factors, but for quality companies that generate strong earnings and return that profit to their shareholders, there is undeniably an underlying value to the share price.

Just pull up a 20-year chart of Apple (AAPL) from 2003 to 2023 (I've included one in Figure 3). All the short-term gyrations start to look like noise. The bigger picture is that a wildly successful company that grows and sustains strong earnings will see the value of its shares increase over time.

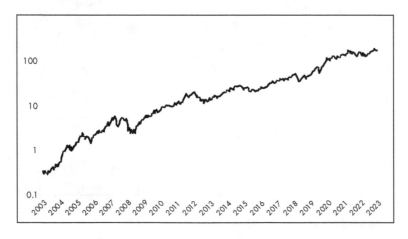

FIGURE 3: APPLE (AAPL)—20YR

Source: Yahoo Finance

Now you are familiar with how stocks are valued and why share prices move.

In the next chapter, we look beyond share prices and highlight a desirable quality of stocks as an asset class—liquidity.

CHAPTER 8:
LIQUIDITY

S USTAINING WEALTH IS a tricky business.

As investors, we look to store our wealth in things that might grow and maintain value, but we diversify because we are aware that any single asset has the potential to fail.

The assets we can choose from—stocks, bonds, land, precious metals, and so on—each have their own pros and cons.

With stocks, dividends and capital gains are how investors make money, but there is another benefit to stocks as an asset class: liquidity.

Liquidity is the ability to quickly and easily swap ownership of an asset for cash.

Being able to turn your wealth into transferable cash is a desirable quality.

If you own undeveloped rural land, it certainly has value, but if a need for cash arises it could take you several months or years to sell the property. It is also hard to estimate exactly what the land is worth until you go through the process of selling it.

The most liquid asset is of course cash itself, but inflation erodes its purchasing power over time, so most long-term savers diversify their wealth into assets that have the ability to maintain *real* value.

What matters is not how much cash you have, but what you can buy with it.

$10 might buy you a cheeseburger today, but if you put $10 under the couch for ten years, and the cost of a burger increases to $20, then you've become poorer.

Keep in mind, the U.S. dollar has lost over 96% of its value since the Federal Reserve System was founded in 1913. It has lost 86% of its value since just 1971 when the U.S. officially abandoned the gold standard (as shown in Figure 4).

We find ourselves in a dilemma. We need cash to *use* our wealth, but we can't hold cash to *keep* our wealth.

The reality of inflation forces savers into non-cash assets, and stocks are one of the most transparent and liquid options.

For the most part, the value of a stock can be ascertained in real-time throughout the day. You can pull up a quote online or call your broker, and with a few clicks or simple instructions you can convert your shares of stock into cash.

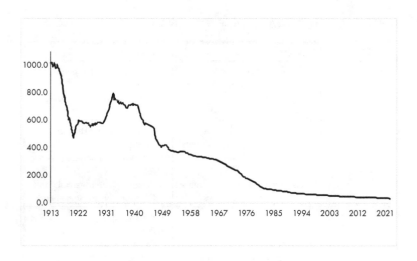

FIGURE 4: PURCHASING POWER OF THE U.S. DOLLAR

Source: U.S. Bureau of Labor Statistics

That flexibility adds to the attractiveness of stocks as a long-term asset. Table 4 indicates some of the pros and cons.

STOCK AS CURRENCY

Investors aren't the only ones that find the liquidity of stocks attractive. Companies can also benefit from having liquid shares of their stock trade on an exchange.

As discussed earlier, as a company grows it often issues equity privately to early employees when it is short on cash and long on promises. Eventually, however, those employees will want to know what their equity is worth, and they'll

TABLE 4: COMMON ASSETS: PROS AND CONS

ASSET	PROS	CONS
Cash	• The most liquid asset • Used as a medium of exchange • Its value is stable day-to-day	• Inflation erodes its purchasing power over time • It does not generate income
Bonds	• Can be converted to cash somewhat quickly depending on the type of bond • Pays interest • Generally less risky than other income producing assets	• Returns may not keep up with inflation • Sensitive to changes in interest rates • Limited upside potential • Company or government risk
Stocks	• Can be converted to cash quickly • A productive asset • Can generate income and returns in excess of inflation • Price transparency	• Price volatility • Price risk • Company risk
Real Estate	• A real asset with limited supply • Can generate income • Can appreciate in price	• Can take long to convert to cash if needed • Little price transparency • Sensitive to interest rates • Can require large upfront payments or the use of debt • Can require maintenance, time, work
Precious Metals	• A real asset with limited supply • Can maintain purchasing power over time • Can be converted to cash quickly in most cases • Price transparency	• An unproductive asset • Does not generate income • Price volatility • Price risk

want the ability to swap it for cash. Having a publicly traded stock will allow them to do so.

Additionally, if a company's stock appreciates in value, the company can use it as a form of currency. For instance, if Meta (META) stock is performing well, CEO Mark

Zuckerberg can issue more of it to pay for high-priced talent, or to make acquisitions, or to build the metaverse.

Using stock-based compensation to lure talented employees was a major trend at Meta and other successful tech companies that saw massive ten-year rallies in their stocks during the 2010s.

At big tech companies like Meta, Google, or Amazon, a senior software engineer might be given a compensation package consisting of a roughly 50/50 mix of cash and stock options.

The **restricted stock units** (**RSUs**), as the stock options are called, are usually based on the company's average stock price around the time the person was hired. If the company's stock marches way higher in an employee's first few years on the job, the RSU portion of their compensation can become very valuable.

But the reverse is also true. If the company's stock plummets during someone's first few years on the job, their stock-based compensation will disappoint.

For example, if someone joined Meta in September 2021, near the peak in its stock price, and was given $100,000 worth of restricted stock units, that portion of their compensation was only worth about $57,000 six months later (see Figure 5).

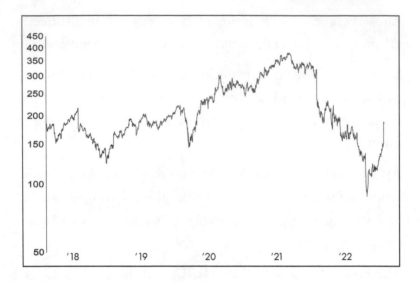

FIGURE 5: META (META)—5YR

Source: FactSet data and analytics

This has two effects: current employees feel like they've gotten a pay cut, and prospective employees think twice about joining the company.

For prospective employees with a contrarian mindset, perhaps there is a chance to *buy the dip*. By going against the grain and joining Meta or some other company while times are tough, a new employee might get more attractively priced stock options.

So, if you happen to be an all-star software engineer whose labor is in high demand, you almost find yourself in the position of an investor—you can choose to chase momentum and join a company whose stock is currently in favor, or you can attempt to see value in what others are selling and join a company that might rebound.

As is always the case with stocks, only time will reveal the right decision.

———

Now we understand the value for both investors and companies in having liquid, publicly traded shares.

In the next chapter, we discuss the process a company follows to get its shares traded on an exchange—"going public," as it's called.

CHAPTER 9:
GOING PUBLIC

I HAD BEEN A regular customer of the Sweetgreen chain of salad restaurants for many years by the time its shares became available to the public.

New locations were popping up all over New York City. The chain was growing rapidly, and I admired how it was run. I could order a fresh salad on their app, and it would be waiting for me on a shelf when I got to the restaurant. It was local, healthy food with the convenience of fast food.

Until 2021, Sweetgreen was a private business, so only insiders—the founders, venture capital, private equity, etc.— could invest in it. But on November 18, 2021, Sweetgreen went public. The stock began trading on the New York Stock Exchange under the ticker symbol SG.

From that day on, I or any person or institution that wanted to invest in Sweetgreen had the ability to do so.

The most common way for a company to make its shares available to the public, like Sweetgreen did, is through an **initial public offering** (**IPO**).

INITIAL PUBLIC OFFERINGS

In an IPO, a company issues new stock to the public. This means that the company creates new shares and sells them to the public for cash. It is therefore a capital-raising event for the company.

The cash raised from the IPO can be used to grow the business. The plans for how the company intends to achieve that growth are outlined in a **prospectus** that is provided to potential investors.

The prospectus is a document that highlights the company's history, financial performance, strategic goals, and plans for the use of investors' cash.

Over the last couple decades, many things in life have become easy, automated processes, but going public through an IPO is certainly not one of them.

The IPO process remains complicated and requires not only an analysis of the company's value, it requires relationships with investors to sell the stock.

If you own a home in a nice neighborhood, you might be able to self-list it on Zillow and attract a bunch of interested buyers. It's not the same for selling a big business.

A company can't just list it on a website and attract the millions or billions of dollars they are looking for.

For these reasons, companies enlist the help of **investment banks** to guide them through the IPO process.

An investment bank will help determine the proper valuation of the company, how many shares of stock should be created, and at what price the shares should be offered. And then, importantly, the investment bank will help introduce the company's management team to its Rolodex of institutional investor clients. It is these institutional investors who provide the bulk of funding for new IPOs.

Investment banks maintain relationships with institutional investors of all sorts—long-only mutual funds, hedge funds, pension funds and so on. The institutional investors pay the investment banks for equity research, access to company management teams, and sometimes prime brokerage services.

BUY-SIDE AND SELL-SIDE

When people talk about Wall Street, they typically divide it into two groups: the **buy-side** and the **sell-side**.

Investments banks are *selling* a service to professional investors, so they are considered part of the sell-side.

The buy-side consists of the professional investors who manage money and pay for, or *buy*, the services provided by investment banks and other sell-side firms.

In the equities division of an investment bank, there are analysts, salespeople, and traders who work on selling IPOs. The analysts will value the company. The salespeople will then pitch the new stock to the institutional investors. And when the salespeople get buyers, the traders will execute the orders.

Typically, several investment banks will play a part in the same IPO. Collectively, the group of banks that finds buyers for the sale of stock is called the **syndicate**.

Each investment bank's compensation and level of involvement in the deal depends on what role they are designated in the process.

Managing the show are the lead underwriters, also known as the **bookrunners**. The lead underwriters assist in the registration and due diligence process, and then lead the selling effort.

Supporting the lead bookrunners are **passive bookrunners** and **co-managers**.

Co-managers play a smaller role but might have investor relationships that are complementary to the big banks, which are usually the leads.

For instance, while the lead underwriter might be able to place big chunks of stock to mega funds like T. Rowe

Price and Fidelity, the co-manager might have relationships with smaller, sector-specialized investors who would like to purchase shares.

Name Drop: bulge bracket banks

On Wall Street, the "bulge brackets" is a term applied to a group of the most well-known, largest, and firmly established investment banks in the world.

The bulge brackets often act as lead underwriters, or bookrunners, on the biggest IPOs.

The following investment banks are commonly included in the bulge bracket grouping:

Goldman Sachs
J.P. Morgan
Morgan Stanley
Deutsche Bank
Credit Suisse
Barclays
UBS
Citigroup
Bank of America

Although this is a prestigious group, these companies are not invincible.

The now-defunct Lehman Brothers and Bear Stearns used to be included in this group. Their investment

---

> banking revenues rivaled those of Goldman Sachs and J.P. Morgan, but both firms collapsed during the Financial Crisis of 2008–2009.

The co-managers are also there to help with post-IPO support for the stock. They generally pick up research coverage of the stock and may facilitate meetings between management and investors after the stock has gone public. The lead bookrunners may or may not pick up research coverage following the IPO transaction.

The typical sequence of events is that after the prospectus is issued to potential investors, the bookrunners will organize a **roadshow**. This is when the company's management team is put in front of investors and given its chance to directly pitch their story. Imagine Shark Tank without the theme song or Mr. Wonderful!

The company's management team will likely have many meetings over the course of one to two weeks. Their aim is to convince big, institutional money managers to purchase their stock. These are discerning investors that have lots of stocks to choose from, so they need to be convinced why a newly public company is worth allocating their dollars to.

Following the investor meetings, the bookrunners will take indications of interest from the money managers. They find out who wants to buy, how much they want to buy, and what price per share they are willing to pay.

This information helps the bookrunners determine an appropriate price for the stock—the **IPO price**.

The IPO price is the price per share that is offered to the institutional investors before the stock starts trading on an exchange.

If there is strong demand for the new shares and the investment bank receives more orders than they can fill, the IPO is said to be **oversubscribed**.

Conversely, if there is weak demand for the new shares and the investment bank does not receive enough orders to meet their target, the IPO is **undersubscribed**.

It is the investment bank's job to find balance in the market. Like the market for any good or service, they can find balance by shifting the IPO price higher or lower—i.e., making the stock cheaper or more expensive.

If the IPO is oversubscribed, the investment bank may be able to increase the IPO price, which means more capital is raised for the issuing company, and potentially more fees are earned for the investment bank.

And if the IPO is undersubscribed, the price could be lowered, so the company might receive less capital and the investment bank might make less money.

Importantly, the investment bank acts as an **underwriter** in the IPO process. This means that the investment bank buys shares from the issuing company and then sells them to the public. As the middleman in the sale, they are taking temporary ownership of the shares, and thereby taking a financial risk.

They also have a reputation to protect. It is in their best interest to have smooth launches. Companies looking to go public in the future will surely want to see a history of successful IPOs from whichever investment bank they choose to lead their process.

With the pressure on, the investment bank finalizes the allocations. They assess all the order requests, and then they determine which investors will receive shares.

This is a subjective process and is not without bias. Big investors who are high paying clients of the investment bank will typically be given priority.

For hot IPOs that attract strong investor interest, it is unlikely that an individual retail investor will get to purchase shares at the IPO price, but it is not impossible.

If you're an individual hoping to get in on an IPO, it is possible that your brokerage was allocated some shares, so you can reach out to them with an indication of interest. If you have some influence there, or just get lucky, you may be able to get your hands on some shares at the IPO price.

The sales of stock that take place at the pre-determined IPO price are known as **primary market sales**.

The primary market is when a company sells new shares of stock and the money paid for the shares goes to the company.

Once the IPO is concluded and the shares have been allocated to investors, all future buying and selling of those shares will take place between participants in the open market, called the **secondary market**.

The issuing company will no longer be involved in the transactions; they will not receive or pay money when their stock is bought and sold on an exchange.

For example, when you log into your brokerage account and purchase shares of Apple (AAPL) stock, you are buying it from some person or institution who owns the stock and wants to sell it. Apple itself has nothing to do with the transaction.

IPO PERFORMANCE

At some point on the day of the IPO, usually a couple hours after the market opens, the stock will begin trading on the exchange. It is off to the races!

Notable companies may get to ring the iconic bell on the floor of the New York Stock Exchange as the first buyer-to-seller trades take place. Financial media will show footage of smiling company founders and executives applauding their accomplishment.

Those smiles, however, don't mean the stock price will grind higher from there. Stocks do not always perform well right out of the gate.

The performance of new stocks is mixed. Some stocks trade at values significantly higher than their IPO price from the very first public trade. But there are other stocks that struggle to even maintain the IPO price at which institutional investors purchased them in the primary market.

It is far from obvious which new stocks will do well on day one.

On May 18, 2012, there was a ton of hype around the Facebook (FB) (now known as Meta (META)) IPO. Facebook was a disruptive, consumer-loved company that garnered a lot of interest from both institutional and retail investors.

Investment bankers set the IPO price at $38 per share. The stock began trading around 11:30am ET and soon shot up to around $45 per share, but then the momentum waned. The stock fell back to the $38 IPO price and struggled to stay there.

In fact, it took an active effort on the part of the lead underwriter, Morgan Stanley, to support the stock above the IPO price.

Bankers can help support the launch of the stock through what's called a **greenshoe option**.

A greenshoe option is a provision in the underwriting agreement that allows the investment bank to sell a certain percentage of extra shares—usually 15%—should there be excess demand.

In the case of Facebook, there initially seemed to be excess demand, so Morgan Stanley chose to take advantage of the greenshoe and distribute (sell) 63 million more shares to investors than was originally planned.

However, buying quickly dried up and the stock fell back down to $38, so Morgan Stanley re-purchased those 63m extra shares back from the public.

This move made Morgan Stanley a big buyer of the stock, providing increased demand, so it was able to help prevent its value falling below the $38 IPO price, at least for the day. Facebook shares closed at $38.23 on its first day of trading.

If the selling pressure is too intense, a stock can fall below the IPO price even with the investment bank's use of the greenshoe option.

Uber Technologies (UBER) is one notable stock that closed below its IPO price on day one. Uber's IPO price was set at $45 by investment bankers, but the stock ended up closing at $41.57 on its first day of trading. That means that institutional investors that were allocated UBER shares in the primary market were sitting on a losing position by the end of the day.

It's not only the first-day performance of IPOs that is questionable. There is data to suggest that newly public shares can underperform for months or even years. However, there is a wide variance in outcomes, so it is difficult to proclaim any broad conclusions about it.

There are some cases where a stock never looks back from its first day of trading. For example, investors who bought Google (GOOGL) shares (now known as Alphabet) on the first day of trading made out well. The stock marched steadily higher in the months following its IPO and never traded back down to its initial price level.

If an investor bought $1,000 worth of Google shares on its first day of trading in 2004 and held it until today (2023), they would be worth over $50,000 (as Figure 6 demonstrates).

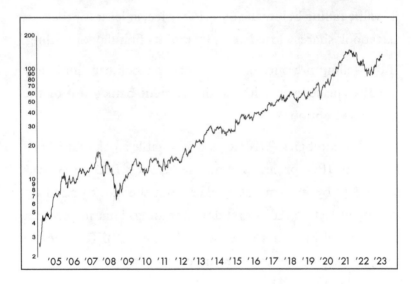

FIGURE 6: ALPHABET (GOOGL)—19YR

Source: FactSet data and analytics

In other cases, IPO stocks have underperformed the broader market by a wide margin. Many stocks that went public during the euphoric market rally of 2021 suffered significant losses the following year.

For example, Traeger, the maker of popular wood pellet grills, went public on July 29, 2021 under the ticker symbol COOK. The stock traded as high as $23.74 that day, but over the next 11 months the stock persistently grinded lower, trading as low as $2.52 on September 2, 2022: an 89% loss for investors who purchased shares on day one (see Figure 7).

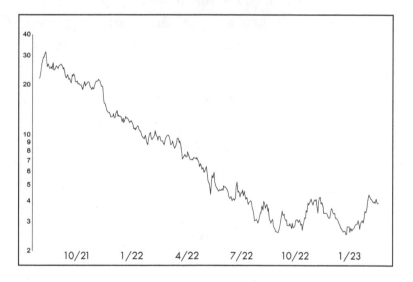

FIGURE 7: TRAEGER (COOK)—2YR

Source: FactSet data and analytics

There are a few sensible theories as to why IPO stocks might underperform initially out of the gate.

The first is that companies decide when they want to go public and raise money. Naturally, they are more inclined to sell shares for cash when the market is euphoric and placing a high valuation on their stock. We saw this in 2021, as a record number of companies went public and raised funds during a boom year in the stock market.

The problem is that booms often turn into busts. Investors who purchase stocks at high valuations during overly optimistic years are prone to suffering drawbacks when reality sets in and valuations revert back toward historical means.

The second reason IPOs might underperform is that insiders—like the founders, owners, early employees, and early investors—are selling while the general public is buying.

As an individual investor, you may be excited when a company you like goes public and you finally get the chance to invest in it. But you must remember, the private investors who have owned the company for a long time are probably even more excited for their chance to ring the register. They are often sitting on big fortunes and take advantage of the opportunity to turn some of their previously illiquid ownership in the company into life-changing cash.

The insiders are typically not allowed to cash out right away. There is a **lock-up period**, usually somewhere between 90–180 days after the IPO, during which insiders can't sell.

But once the lock-up period expires, company insiders can sell their shares in the open market. These insiders sometimes own large chunks of stock, and their selling can put downward pressure on the share price.

OTHER WAYS TO GO PUBLIC

The IPO is the most common way for a company to get its shares listed and trading on an exchange, but it is not the only option.

A **direct listing** is an alternative option for companies that want to have their shares trade on an exchange but don't need to raise capital. While an IPO is a money-raising event for companies, a direct listing is not.

In a direct listing, which is also referred to as a **direct placement** or **direct public offering** (**DPO**), a company does not issue new shares in exchange for cash. Rather, the shares that the insiders already own become tradable on the exchange—the insiders are the sellers from day one.

As with an IPO, companies that go public via a direct listing must meet certain requirements and file a registration statement with the SEC. But since a direct listing does not require an underwriter, it is a cheaper way for a company to go public. It also offers insiders a quicker path to selling their shares since there is no lock-up period.

Some notable companies that went public via direct listing instead of an IPO were Warby Parker, Spotify, Roblox, and Coinbase.

An alternative way to go public is through a **special purpose acquisition company,** or **SPAC** as it is usually called.

SPACs became all the rage during the bubbly market of 2021, but they have since attracted a high degree of criticism and distrust from investors.

With a SPAC, money is raised by a sponsor, who is typically someone with a big reputation. It can be a hot-shot money manager or even a celebrity from an industry outside of finance like sports or entertainment.

The sponsor uses their name to raise funds, promising their investors that they will make an attractive acquisition when the opportunity presents itself. The sponsor essentially receives a blank check from investors to do with as they please.

The SPAC will trade on an exchange under a temporary ticker symbol while the SPAC sponsor searches for an acquisition. If they don't find a suitable company to purchase, the money gets returned to investors and the SPAC is decommissioned.

If the sponsor does find a suitable acquisition target, they will use the funds to purchase a minority stake in the company.

Shareholders in the SPAC then vote to approve the SPAC's merger with the real company that it is acquiring. If the vote passes, the SPAC entity dissolves (a process known as a de-SPAC), and the real company is left trading on the exchange under its own new ticker symbol.

For example, in the spring of 2021 a SPAC was formed called Marquee Raine Acquisition Corporation. It was a shell company trading under the ticker symbol MRAC.

Later in the year, MRAC acquired Enjoy Technologies, which was an in-the-home retail service run by a well-known former Sears CEO, Ron Jonson. When the merger was approved, the entity de-SPAC'd and Enjoy Technologies began trading as a standalone company under the ticker symbol ENJY.

Essentially, a SPAC amounts to a backdoor way for companies to go public. Some companies argue that it is a quicker way to go public and raise funds with fewer regulatory hurdles.

Many investors bought into the hype around SPACs, and they became popular in the speculative mania of 2021. As the year went on and the momentum in the broader stock market waned, investors wised up to some of a SPAC's drawbacks—like high fees, a lack of regulatory oversight, and dilution (i.e., the issuance of additional stock, thereby reducing the ownership proportion of a current shareholder).

In many cases, the SPAC sponsors made a lot of money without risking much of their own capital, while the retail investors who bought shares in the SPACs got burned.

Overall, the performance of SPACs has been lousy.

Enjoy Technologies (ENJY) is certainly not representative of all SPACs, but it filed for bankruptcy less than a year after its public debut. It's a good reminder that just because a company goes public, it does not mean that their business is running on solid ground.

Now we know how a company's stock goes public.

Once it launches, the share price is determined by buyers and sellers in the open market.

That market, where buyers and sellers meet to trade shares, is what people call "the stock market."

In the next part of this book, we discuss how the stock market works.

PART THREE: THE STOCK MARKET

A COMPANY'S STOCK GOES public. It's exciting!

Like pressing send on a tweet—it's now out there for the world to judge. Only, the stock gets voted on with dollars rather than with likes and mean comments.

The stock now trades freely, moving higher or lower in price as both individuals and institutions buy it or sell it as they wish.

A lot of analysis can go into what a stock is worth, but ultimately its price is determined by supply and demand.

A company can report great earnings results, but if there are more sellers than buyers at that moment, the stock can still fall in price.

There are no concrete analytical rules for determining a stock's price. You can come up with an estimate of what you *think* it's worth, but the actual price of a stock is what someone is willing to pay for it.

A stock is an asset just like other things of value that people can own and sell. And people have various reasons for deciding to buy or sell something.

Their decision could be based on emotion or some life situation they're going through. Their decision could be based on a misguided view, or even a correct view that's just ahead of its time. The reasons that people decide to buy and sell things are not always rational, but that doesn't make them less real.

That's part of the beauty of the stock market. You don't need to give a reason when you hit the buy or sell button. No explanations are necessary from either party in the trade.

Unlike some other fields, like politics, in the realm of stocks all expert opinions eventually get judged against a hard objective reality: the price. You can argue all you want that the market is wrong, but your profit & loss (P&L) is an objective scorecard.

The place where buyers and sellers determine stock prices is the **secondary market**, or as most people call it—the **stock market**.

CHAPTER 10:
EXCHANGES

W HEN PEOPLE SPEAK in general about the stock market, they are usually referring broadly to all the major stock exchanges.

Stock exchanges are the organized markets where shares of stocks are bought and sold.

We commonly think of the stock market as a single entity, but it is in fact made up of several different exchanges, each with its own operations, requirements, fees, incentives, and so on.

The two major exchanges in the United States are the **New York Stock Exchange** (**NYSE**) and the **Nasdaq Stock Market**.

Nasdaq stands for National Association of Securities Dealers Automated Quotation System. The full name is a mouthful, so it's almost always referred to by its acronym, Nasdaq.

Together, the New York Stock Exchange and the Nasdaq account for most of the stock trading in the United States.

If you are a typical individual investor submitting relatively small buy and sell orders through a brokerage account, it won't make much of a difference whether a stock is listed on the NYSE or Nasdaq. Your experience in buying or selling the stock will be the same regardless of its listed exchange.

However, a lot goes on underneath the hood of the broker's user-friendly website. There are notable differences not just between the two big exchanges, but also other alternative trading venues like independent electronic communications networks (ECNs) and dark pools, which we will address later in this chapter.

As for the New York Stock Exchange versus the Nasdaq, their respective origins are quite representative of their differences.

The New York Stock Exchange is the storied original. It was founded in 1792 and is the oldest American stock exchange still in existence. It is the largest equities-based exchange in the world based on the total market capitalization of its listed securities.

The New York Stock Exchange has historically been associated with "blue chip" companies, which are big, well-established, companies with strong reputations.

The NYSE is known for including many traditional economy companies in industries like financials, industrials, and energy. Some of the companies listed on the NYSE have long legacies, like J.P. Morgan Chase, Caterpillar, and ExxonMobil. These are the old American titans of industry.

The Nasdaq, on the other hand, is the young buck. It was founded in 1971 as the first fully electronic marketplace for buying and selling stocks. While the NYSE is still bigger in terms of total market cap, the Nasdaq is the leader in sheer volume of shares traded.

Consistent with its founding as an innovative technology platform, the Nasdaq is typically associated with technology-related growth companies. Generally, the new-age growth companies found on the Nasdaq skew smaller in size. There are of course exceptions, as tech companies like Apple, Alphabet, and Amazon have become some of the biggest companies in the world.

It is cheaper for a company to list on the Nasdaq than on the NYSE, which is a meaningful incentive for smaller growth companies that aren't yet generating profit.

The entry fee for a company to be listed on the New York Stock Exchange can be as high as $250,000. Whereas, at the time of this writing, the entry fee for a company to be listed on the Nasdaq is between $50,000 to $75,000.

Subsequent annual fee requirements vary based on share count and other factors, but generally the annual fee requirements are also cheaper on the Nasdaq.

Operationally, the main difference between the two exchanges is that the NYSE is an auction market while the Nasdaq is a dealer's market.

An **auction market** is like it sounds—an auction. Think of an auction for antiques or collectibles. A transaction occurs between the seller of the item and the buyer who is willing to pay the most, with a person who oversees the process.

At the NYSE, this person overseeing the process used to be called a specialist but is now referred to as a **designated market maker** (**DMM**). The designated market maker's job is to facilitate an orderly market.

If trading is running smoothly, the DMM may just observe the action and let the buyers and sellers function on their own. If, however, volatility picks up and there is a lack of buyers or sellers in a given stock, the designated market maker is obligated to step in and be a buyer or seller when needed.

A **dealer's market**, as run by the Nasdaq, is also like it sounds—a dealership. Think of a dealership for used cars. The dealership keeps an inventory of used cars. If you go to a dealership to buy or sell a car, your transaction will occur with the dealer rather than the previous or next driver of the car.

That's sort of how it works at the Nasdaq, which has designated **dealers** for each stock who post prices at which they would buy or sell it.

The dealer acts as a **market maker** who actively buys and sells stocks on behalf of traders. The dealer is a member firm or market participant such as a brokerage company or bank. For a company to list its shares on the Nasdaq, it must have a minimum of three dealers for its stock.

While the processes differ somewhat, the NYSE's designated market maker and the Nasdaq's dealer have the same aim—to facilitate a smooth and orderly market for buyers and sellers of stocks. There is no clear advantage of one over the other.

Both exchanges require that their listed companies provide regular financial reports, audited earnings, and maintain minimum capital requirements.

Most of the smaller stock exchanges in the United States have been consolidated by the two gorillas—the NYSE and the Nasdaq.

For example, the Chicago Stock Exchange was acquired in 2018 by Intercontinental Exchange, which is the parent company that owns the NYSE, and the Boston and Philadelphia stock exchanges are now owned by Nasdaq.

There are many stock exchanges outside of the United States. Some of the major ones include the London Stock Exchange, Euronext, the Shanghai Stock Exchange, the Tokyo Stock Exchange, and the Hong Kong Stock Exchange.

EVOLVING MARKETS

Technology has had a profound effect on the stock market's evolution.

The first modern form of stock trading was created in Amsterdam in 1611. The Dutch East India Company was the first publicly traded company, and for many years, it was the only company with trading activity on the exchange.

Even by the year 1800, only a handful of stocks were actively trading in major business centers like London. It was slow and costly to trade stocks. People wrote with feathered pens, and paper was expensive.

It wasn't until well into the 19th century that the development of cheap carbon paper, typewriters, and printed forms made it possible to do business as we know it.

In 1837, Samuel Morse invented the telegraph, which revolutionized long-distance communication. And then 30 years later, building off that technology, Thomas Edison created the ticker machine.

The ticker machine was like a computer printer that only printed stock tickers and prices on a thin piece of paper. A fun fact: the tape was constantly running and would pile up at brokers' offices who needed to get rid of it, so they used the ticker tape as confetti at parades, which is the origin of the *ticker tape parade*.

Technology continued to advance over the next century and created new efficiencies in stock trading.

By the time of the computer revolution in the second half of the 20th century, it was becoming inevitable that our exchanges would be underpinned by the speed of light.

From the 1970s through the 1990s, we saw the rise of **electronic communications networks**, or **ECNs**.

Originally, ECNs were like electronic bulletin boards. They were not exchanges, but rather a place where people who were interested in buying or selling shares could post their interest.

This was especially relevant for institutional investors looking to fill big orders. If an investor didn't want to advertise a large, cut-and-dry order on the proper exchanges for the whole world to see, they could instead post their interest on the ECN bulletin board and describe the conditions under which they'd make a trade. It became a popular alternative to the main exchanges with institutional investors.

The SEC allowed these websites to function as ECNs, a distinct classification different from an exchange. But as time went on, the ECNs started to look more like exchanges. As the speed and cost advantages of ECN trading attracted more customers, the NYSE and Nasdaq began to see the ECNs as worrisome competition.

If you can't beat them, buy them!

Two of the most popular ECNs, Instinet and Archipelago, were acquired within a week of each other in 2005 by Nasdaq and NYSE, respectively.

OVER THE COUNTER (OTC)

Not all companies can meet the listing requirements of the exchanges.

These companies, which are often smaller and riskier, are known as **pink sheets** and can have their shares trade **over the counter** (**OTC**).

Instead of trading on a centralized, formal exchange like the NYSE or the Nasdaq, their shares trade dealer to dealer.

In case you're curious, pink sheets received their name because the listings for these OTC stocks used to be printed on pink paper. Today, they are published electronically and called OTC pink.

Most pink sheet listings are low-priced stocks, meaning their share prices are below $5. Sometimes pink sheet stocks will trade for as low as one penny, which is why they are often referred to as **penny stocks**.

Pink sheet stocks are highly speculative. There is sometimes little disclosure or data on these companies, so while it is possible to find a diamond in the rough, there are also scams that could result in investors losing all their money. The SEC warns that pink sheets are among the riskiest investments given the lack of regulation or oversight on the securities.

Imagine you go to a suspicious auto dealership that sells thousands of well-known cars at cheap prices. But you are not interested in these well-known cars that you see on the lot. You instead ask the salesperson if they have a used, worn-down 1992 Mitsubishi Galant. He responds, "We definitely don't have that here, but I might know a guy who does."

He walks off into the corner of the room and makes a phone call, then comes back and says, "I can get it for you for $5,000."

You don't really know how he's getting it or if the price is fair or if the car will even perform, but you'll be able to buy it. That's how I think about pink sheet stocks.

DELISTINGS

In some cases, legitimate companies that are listed on a major exchange hit hard times and fail. If a listed company is no longer able to meet the requirements for continued listing on the NYSE or Nasdaq, it will be **delisted**.

Delistings usually happen to companies that are under significant financial strain and near bankruptcy.

These delisted stocks will become listed on the **over-the-counter bulletin board** (**OTCBB**).

The main difference between the OTCBB and pink sheets is that OTCBB companies are still required to maintain SEC filings and minimum reporting requirements set by the Financial Industry Regulatory Authority (FINRA) and the OTCBB. The requirements are considerably easier to meet than those set by the national exchanges.

If you own the stock of a company that declares bankruptcy, you will likely see its listing transferred to the OTCBB and a letter "Q" will be added to the end of its ticker symbol.

For example, when General Motors declared bankruptcy on June 1, 2009, the old shares were delisted from the New York Stock Exchange on June 2. The original shares that were listed under the symbol GM began trading on the OTCBB as Motors Liquidation Company, ticker GMGMQ.

As an owner of bankrupt shares, you can either attempt to sell them, likely for a significant loss, or you can hold them. As the bankruptcy proceedings play out, the shares could likely go to $0 and cease trading. However, until it is all said and done, there is always a small chance that the future post-reorganization value will exceed the currently depressed share price.

But betting on bankrupt companies is a very high-risk gamble. Even if a company does reorganize under bankruptcy law and continue to operate, in many instances the creditors and lenders will become the new owners and the plan for reorganization will effectively cancel the existing shares—making them worthless.

Personal story: the transformation of markets

Financial markets have undergone an astonishing technological transformation over the last few decades.

In the early 1800s, members of the New York Stock Exchange met in coffee shops in lower Manhattan to trade shares. They later rented a room at 40 Wall Street, where brokers gathered twice a day to trade a list of 30 stocks and bonds.

Fast forward to today, and millions of shares trade in thousands of stocks at lightning speed on electronic screens. It is a remarkable change in just two centuries.

Commodities markets have undergone similar change. I witnessed part of the electronification first-hand.

In 2005 I worked as an intern at the New York Mercantile Exchange (NYMEX), which was one of the world's major commodity futures exchanges.

I sat in the middle of a circular pit wearing protective eyeglasses, as screaming natural gas traders tossed index cards at my face.

The traders would shout buy and sell orders at each other across the pit. This was known as the **open outcry system.** When they verbally agreed on a trade, the details were handwritten on a paper card and thrown to someone, like me, sitting in the middle of the pit who would timestamp the card and hand it over for processing.

There was another nearly as prestigious job, called the runner, who took the timestamped cards and physically ran them to the operations team in the back office for clearing.

By 2009, within just four years of my first day at the exchange, the yelling traders were all gone. The trading room, known as the floor, had become an empty ghost town.

Trading could now be done through a computer, so there was no need to be there. Some of the traders I knew from the floor started working from home, others rented offices, and others quit trading altogether.

It was the end of one era, and the beginning of a new one.

The NYMEX officially closed its trading pits at the end of 2016. It still operates electronically, under the ownership of CME Group.

OUT OF THE SPOTLIGHT

There is no rule that stock trades can only occur on the major exchanges. That freedom to trade enabled the rise of ECNs as an alternative trading system (ATS), and it has also enabled the growth of so-called **dark pools**.

A dark pool is a privately organized financial forum or exchange for trading securities. The name sounds ominous, like it is an illegal black market, but dark pools are in fact regulated by the SEC.

What's unique about dark pools is that they are anonymous and not open to the public. No one can see who is buying and selling.

Why might someone want to remain anonymous when shopping a buy or sell order?

If you are a big player who trades a lot of shares, your actions can move the market.

For example, if a big pension fund is looking to sell $1bn of Starbucks (SBUX) stock, that degree of selling pressure could temporarily push the price lower. A big chunk of stock like that is called a **block**. There's not always a buyer standing ready to purchase a large block of stock.

If the pension fund were to post the large sell order for everyone to see on a regular exchange, smaller traders might try to front run the order—selling their own stock before the big block finds a buyer—pushing down the price.

Since the pension fund wants the best (highest) price for the stock it is selling, it may instead look to anonymously gauge interest for its shares in a dark pool. It might be able to find a buyer in the dark pool without risking any disturbance to the share price based on its intent.

If they do find a buyer and make a trade in the dark pool, they'll have to disclose the sale after it's done, but it'll be too late for any front running.

Some traders monitor the positions of big funds as a gauge on sentiment. If a respected investor like Warren Buffett dumps a stock, it could be viewed as a lack of confidence in the company and the shares might fall after the transaction is disclosed. Conversely, if he takes a new position in a stock, it could be seen as an endorsement of the company and the shares might rally.

In any case, if you're a big or influential investor, you can move the market—whether you want to or not—so anonymity can be valuable.

Whale watching: 13F holdings reports

Imagine the smartest students in school had to share their test answers with the rest of the class.

It would be very helpful to the lower-performing students if the answers were shared in real-time, but not so helpful if the answers were shared after the exam was over.

That's kind of how investors view 13F filings.

The SEC requires that institutional investors with at least $100m in assets under management

(AUM) disclose their equities holdings quarterly by filing a Form 13F.

Funds are required to file Form 13F within 45 days after the last day of the calendar quarter. Most of them wait until the end of the period in order to conceal their moves as long as possible.

While it's interesting to see what moves the smart money is making, the data can be somewhat stale, reflecting investments already over four months old.

Fast-moving hedge funds could already be out of a trade by the time the public sees it. The disclosures can be somewhat more relevant for long-only investors that typically own stocks for many years.

There have been some concerns raised about dark pools because they suck some liquidity away from the public eye of the main exchanges.

Since big trades are happening out of sight of the general public, there is a sense that the exchanges aren't showing the whole picture of what's going on in the market.

There is also a concern that high-frequency trading firms could be taking advantage of price discrepancies between the dark pools and the other exchanges.

High-frequency trading involves the use of algorithms and ultra-high-speed internet connections that allow computer trading programs to react and place orders faster than any human.

In theory, the high-frequency trading firm could detect someone's buy order, then beat them to the punch and buy the stock first, only to sell it back to the buyer for a slightly higher price.

Imagine that you and I are sitting at the kitchen table.

I see you start to reach for the last slice of pizza, so I throw my arm out and grab it first. I then tell you that I'll give you the slice, but only if you give me a few of your potato chips.

That's the idea behind **front running**.

High-frequency trading firms will argue that they are valuable providers of liquidity in the market. They help orders get filled quickly, and they increase competition for orders in the market, which ultimately improves the trading experience for both individuals and institutions.

It's a debate for regulators.

———

Now you understand *where* stocks trade.

In the next chapter, we describe *how* stocks trade. We will highlight the process and terminology involved in buying and selling shares.

CHAPTER 11:
HOW STOCKS TRADE

A FARMER'S MARKET MATCHES buyers and sellers.

There's a seller of bread, a seller of eggs, and a seller of lettuce—each asking for a specific price.

There are also buyers of these things, each with a limit to what they'll spend.

A price discovery process unfolds, be it via direct haggling between the buyers and sellers, or simply by the sellers adjusting prices in response to buyers' behavior.

When a seller and buyer agree on a specific item at a specific price, a transaction is made and ownership is transferred.

Essentially, that's how stocks trade too.

Running a stock exchange is certainly more complex than managing a farmer's market—there are significant operational, compliance, legal, and technological hurdles to overcome—but the end result is similar. The aim of both is to efficiently match buyers and sellers.

In the stock market, an order to purchase shares of stock is called a **bid**, and an order to sell shares of stock is called an **ask**.

It is similar to buying a home. The seller will *ask* for a price, and then interested buyers will submit their *bids*. Where the bid meets the ask, a sale occurs.

Before the rise of online brokerages, an investor had to call their broker on the phone to give an order to buy or sell a stock. The broker would then charge a pricey commission for executing the trade as payment for the service.

Now, thanks to the internet and good old capitalistic competition, it couldn't be easier to use an online broker and submit your own orders through the broker's website. Many of the reputable online brokers today charge no commission on trades.

Nothing is free: zero-commission brokers

The online brokers offering free trades are not doing it out of charity. In many cases, they are getting paid for order flow.

Payment for order flow is when a brokerage company has an agreement with a third-party company to direct its customer orders their way in exchange for a commission or fee based on volume.

Why would a third-party want to pay for the broker's orders?

It comes back to the dark pools mentioned in the last chapter.

If you submit an order to buy stock through an online broker, like TD Ameritrade or Robinhood, your order is not necessarily routed to a main exchange like Nasdaq or NYSE to be matched with a seller.

It is more likely that your zero-commission broker sends the order to a wholesaler that operates in the dark pools.

The wholesaler might be able to get you a good price, but it might not be the *best* price.

As a middleman in the process, the wholesaler can profit by making sure its average buys in a stock are lower than its average sells. The profit may only be a couple pennies per share, but if the wholesaler facilitates millions of trades, the pennies of profit will add up.

So, if you use a commission-free broker, the free trades can be nice, but just realize that you may be incurring indirect costs, like paying a slightly higher price per share for stocks you buy, and receiving a slightly lower price per share for stocks you sell.

It is also worth being aware that if your broker is getting paid for order flow, they have a financial incentive to entice you into placing more trades.

Unless you are a very skilled short-term trader, overtrading, or **churn**, is usually detrimental to your returns. Be wary of any gamification or gimmickry on your broker's app that incentivizes frequent trading.

SUBMITTING ORDERS

When you walk up to the apple stand at the farmer's market and the sign says, "Apples $2 each," there are two ways you could proceed.

You could either hand over the $2 and take your apple. Or you could tell the farmer that you're only willing to give him $1.75 and see what he says. Maybe he will sell it to you, maybe he won't.

Your options are similar when placing an order to purchase shares of stock, only there's specific terminology that's used.

In order to identify the terms while also highlighting the order-placing process in which they are used, we will walk through the steps of submitting a trade through an online broker.

The user interface will vary a bit between different brokerage companies, but the process for placing a trade will be similar.

On my online broker's home screen, a tab titled "Trade" brings me to an order screen where I can buy and sell stocks.

There are six boxes that need to be filled out to submit the order. That sounds like a lot, but it can be done in only a few seconds once you're familiar with the process.

Action

The first box is titled "Action." This is where you identify what you are trying to do.

There is a dropdown menu providing these options: 1) Buy, 2) Sell, 3) Buy to Cover, and 4) Sell Short.

Buy and *Sell* are straightforward. For most ordinary long-term investors, these are the only two options you will ever need.

Buy to Cover and *Sell Short* involve short selling, which is a risky practice that involves betting on a stock to go down in price, as mentioned in Chapter 5.

In this hypothetical example, I will be buying stock, so I select *Buy*.

Symbol

The second box is titled "Symbol." This is where you identify the stock you are looking to trade by entering its **ticker symbol**.

As mentioned in Chapter 4, the ticker symbol is usually related to the company in some way. For example, Spotify is SPOT, J.P. Morgan is JPM, and Dollar General is DG.

In this example, I will buy shares of Apple, whose ticker symbol is AAPL.

When I type AAPL into the box, a real-time price quote pops up for shares of Apple. It tells me that right now the bid is $151.07, and the ask is $151.09—meaning that someone is willing to buy shares for $157.07 per share, and someone is willing to sell shares for $151.09 per share.

The bid and ask are the highest and lowest prices participants in the market are willing to trade for, respectively. The difference between the bid and ask is known as the **spread**.

In well-known stocks where a lot of volume trades each day, the difference between the bid and ask is very small—like in this case, it is only two cents. For smaller, less liquid stocks the spread will usually be wider.

Quantity

The third box is "Quantity." This is where you indicate how many shares you want to buy or sell.

In this example, I would like to invest about $600 in Apple shares. Since the seller is asking for $151.09 per share, I can purchase four shares for $604.36. That's close enough to the $600 I wanted to invest, so I enter 4 as the quantity of shares.

Recent feature: fractional shares

Some brokers now offer the option to trade **fractional shares**, which allows investors to purchase or sell less than one full share.

If my broker offered fractional shares, and I really wanted to invest exactly $600, I could submit a trade to purchase $600 worth of AAPL and I would receive about 3.7 shares instead of 4 full shares.

If you purchase fractional shares, you are treated the same as someone who owns full shares. Your position in the stock will experience the same percentage gains or losses as a full share.

And if the stock pays a dividend, you will receive a payment based on how many shares you own, just as any other investor would. For example, if shareholders receive a $2 dividend for each share they own and you own a half share, you receive $1.

Fractional shares can be useful for small investors who want to invest in a company but don't have enough money to purchase a full share.

> One potential disadvantage of owning fractional shares is that you may not have voting rights. Additionally, trading rules, costs, and fees can vary between brokers, so investors should make sure they're not paying unnecessarily more for the feature.

Order type

The fourth box is "Order type." This gets back to the apple stand at the farmer's market. Do you want to buy at the asking price or do you want to haggle?

A **market order** means that you will just buy your shares at the asking price. You give the seller what they are asking for. No haggling.

In this case, the seller is asking for $151.09, so if I select to purchase using a market order, I will pay $151.09 per share.

In a stock like Apple with an only two-cent spread between the bid and ask, there's probably no need to fight for a penny.

When I purchase stocks for long-term investment, I usually use a market order as long as the bid-ask spread is reasonable. For the well-known types of companies that I typically invest in, the spread is usually never more than a few pennies.

If you want to haggle for a better price, then you can place a **limit order**.

With a limit order, you can submit a buy or sell order—a bid or ask—at a specific price. In this example, AAPL is being offered at $151.09 per share, but perhaps I only want to buy shares if the price falls lower. I might, for instance, only be willing buy shares at $150.50, but no more than that.

If that's the case, I could submit a limit order for 4 shares at $150.50. If the market softens and the stock trades down to $150.50, my order will be filled. However, if the stock keeps marching higher in price from when I submitted my low bid, my order will not get filled.

If it's not filled by the end of the day, the order will be cancelled, and I would need to resubmit a new order the next day if I was still inclined to make the same trade.

For ordinary investors, market orders and limit orders are likely the only two types of orders you will ever need.

For shorter-term traders, there are two additional, more tactical order types that can sometimes be useful: stop orders and trailing stops.

A **stop order**, also called a **stop loss**, is used for setting a maximum loss on a trade.

The goal of a good trader is to have their winning trades be on average bigger than their losing trades.

I remember being shocked as a young trader to hear that some of the best traders are only right on a little over half their trades. They are basically wrong as often as they are right, but they are disciplined in their risk management and ensure that when they are wrong, they limit the losses.

One way to help limit losses is to define upfront the price at which you would cut the losing trade. For example, a trader might come to the view, for whatever reason, that Etsy (ETSY) shares are going to go from $100 to $130 over the next few months. If she's right, that would be a 30% gain on the trade.

However, if she's wrong, as she is half the time, she wants to limit the losses and live to fight another day. So, she might buy the stock at $100 and then place a stop order to sell at $93, indicating that she is only willing to lose 7% on the trade.

If the stock never trades down to $93, the stop order will never be executed. But if the stock does trade down to $93, it will trigger an automatic sell order and the shares will be sold as close to $93 as possible.

It should be noted that a stop order at $93 does not guarantee she will be able to sell her shares at $93. If only it were that easy!

Sometimes a company's shares will gap down following negative news or a disappointing earnings report. If Etsy reports lackluster earnings after the market closes, and it opens the next day trading at $85, she will have to sell it there or cross her fingers and hope that it rallies back up to $93. Most successful traders don't rely on hope.

A **trailing stop order** is similar to a regular stop order, but it is dynamic. It can be set to move with the price of the stock.

For example, suppose the trader bought ETSY shares at $100 and the stock quickly rose to $115. It hasn't yet reached her $130 price target, but she is wary of giving back a winning trade, so she could set a trailing stop order with a parameter of $3.

This means that whenever the stock falls $3 from its high, it will trigger a market order to sell. For example, if the stock rallies from $115 to $120 per share, her trailing stop will rise from $112 to $117, remaining $3 below the new high price.

A trailing stop order can allow the trader to ride the momentum higher but ensure a winning trade by selling as soon as the upward momentum breaks.

Price

The fifth box on the screen is "Price." This applies to limit orders, where you define the price at which you'd like to buy or sell shares.

If you are placing a market order, you do not need to enter a price.

Time in force

The sixth and final box is "Time in force." This clarifies the timing of your order.

The standard selection for this box would be a "Day." A **day order** means that your order to buy or sell shares would be filled during normal market orders that same day, or else not at all.

Markets in the U.S. are open Monday through Friday, 9:30am to 4:00pm ET, excluding market holidays.

If your day order doesn't get filled by 4:00pm ET on the day it's placed, it will be canceled.

You also have the option to submit what's called a **Good-Til-Cancelled order** (**GTC**). A GTC order is an order to buy or sell a stock that lasts until the order is either completed or you indicate to cancel it. It does not automatically cancel at the end of the day.

Brokerage firms typically limit the length of time an investor can leave a GTC order open. The time frame may vary from broker to broker.

———

Now you know how shares of stock are bought and sold.

In the next chapter, we will look beyond individual companies and their share prices. We will discuss groupings of stocks, known as indexes, that provide a more comprehensive picture of how the broader stock market is performing.

CHAPTER 12:
INDEXES

W HEN YOU HEAR that the stock market has been strong, or that the stock market has been weak, that statement is usually based on the price of an index.

An **index** tracks the performance of a certain group of stocks.

A single stock can move way up or way down for any number of company-specific reasons. The CEO may have quit, a patent may have expired, a new product may have gone viral. Regardless of the reason, it's hard to draw broad, market-wide conclusions from the price action of a single stock.

The price action of a basket of stocks, however, can tell a bigger story.

If Apple (AAPL) is down 10% in a week, maybe the new iPhone launch disappointed. But if a basket of the 100 biggest technology companies in the United States is down 10% in a week, it's a significant tide shift and perhaps a warning sign that something bad is brewing in either financial or economic markets.

There are three major indexes in the United States: the Dow Jones Industrial Average, the Standard & Poor's 500, and the Nasdaq Composite (a name you may recognize from the discussion on exchanges).

Each one has its own formula for determining which companies are included in the basket and how much weight is given to each stock. Each of these three indexes tells a different story.

The **Dow Jones Industrial Average**, often shortened to the Dow, tracks 30 of the largest companies in the United States. These are renowned, blue chip companies like Walmart (WMT), Coca-Cola (KO), and J.P. Morgan Chase (JPM). The Dow includes companies across all industries except for utilities and transports.

The Dow is probably the most vernacularly referenced index among the general public. When someone asks how the market did today, they're often referring to how the Dow performed. Collectively, the 30 titans of industry that comprise the Dow provide an illuminating read on the U.S. market as a whole.

I grew up looking at the Dow. By habit it's the first price I check in the morning.

The Dow is a price-weighted index, meaning that the movements of the highest-priced stocks have the greatest impact on the index's value.

Many of the other indexes are weighted by market capitalization rather than price, meaning the size of the company matters more than the price of its shares.

The **Standard & Poor's 500** (**S&P 500**) is a market-cap-weighted index that tracks 500 of the leading U.S. publicly traded companies.

While the Dow gets the most public attention, professional investors usually pay more attention to the S&P 500 because it includes far more companies. It therefore provides a more representative read on how the U.S. stock market is performing.

The S&P 500 is primarily a large-cap index, but its composition is not strictly limited to the 500 biggest companies in the country. The stocks in the index are chosen by a committee at the Standard & Poor's investment company. The committee meets regularly to assess companies based on size, liquidity, and group representation.

Since the S&P 500 consists of 500 leading companies across all sectors, the index is by nature an attractive set-it-and-forget-it investment vehicle. For this reason, investment funds that track the S&P 500 are a popular way to invest in the U.S. stock market.

In recent years, the S&P 500 has become more heavily weighted to technology stocks than it historically had been, but that's in part reflective of the current reality. Technology companies like Apple, Alphabet, and Microsoft have become some of the biggest, most profitable companies in the world.

As of 2022, the information technology sector accounted for 28% of the S&P 500, more than any other sector. That was not always the case. If you went back a couple decades there would have been greater emphasis on consumer discretionary and communications companies. Even further back, you'd find greater emphasis on financials, energy, and industrials.

The S&P 500 index evolves with the U.S. economy. As our economy changes, so will the sector composition of the index.

The **Nasdaq Composite**, on the other hand, has always been a technology-focused index. The Nasdaq Composite includes all the equity securities listed on the Nasdaq Stock Market, which at the time of this writing is more than 3,700 companies.

Since its inception, the Nasdaq exchange has been known for mostly listing technology stocks, so the Nasdaq Composite index is considered a good gauge for how the technology sector is performing.

Like the S&P 500, the Nasdaq Composite index is market-cap weighted. This means that big companies like Apple, Microsoft, and Alphabet have more influence on the index's value than smaller companies.

Unlike the S&P 500 and the Dow Jones Industrial Average, the Nasdaq Composite includes companies headquartered outside of the United States.

In that sense it is a more globally inclusive index. However, many of the biggest U.S. corporations have significant business operations all over the world. Companies like Coca-Cola, McDonald's, and Nike are U.S.-based companies, but at this point they are truly global investments.

When you turn on a financial media network like CNBC, you will often see prices for the Dow, the S&P 500, and the Nasdaq changing in real time on the screen. In a quick glance, these three indexes show you how the blue chips are performing, how the broader market is performing, and how the tech sector is performing.

A fourth index that some investors monitor is the **Russell 2000**. The Russell 2000 tracks the performance of 2,000 smaller companies. It is a good gauge for how small- to mid-cap stocks are performing.

Small-cap companies are companies with market capitalization values ranging from $250m to $2bn. Mid-cap companies are those valued in the $2bn to $10bn range. And large-cap companies are those valued at $10bn or more.

The Dow, S&P 500, and Nasdaq are large-cap heavy, so the Russell 2000 gives you a somewhat different perspective on what's driving the market.

There are periods where small- and mid-cap stocks can significantly outperform or underperform large-cap stocks.

Paying attention to smaller companies can shed some light on what's going on under the hood of the market.

Are innovative, emerging companies propelling the economy forward? Or are the big just getting bigger?

The relative performance of the Russell 2000 can help you answer that question.

PERFORMANCE

The major U.S. indexes have performed incredibly well over time.

As the ubiquitous disclaimer notes, "past performance is not indicative of future performance," but let's look at how these indexes have done.

The performance of the Dow Jones, S&P 500, and Nasdaq are generally correlated.

You can see in Figure 8's 25-year chart, even though the Nasdaq showed some outperformance in the last decade, the three indexes are directionally similar in their movements.

That's because stocks generally tend to move in tandem.

In what's known as a **bull market**, most stocks move higher in price. And in **bear markets** most stocks move lower in price.

Bull and bear are two very commonly used terms in the investment industry. The origin of their use to describe

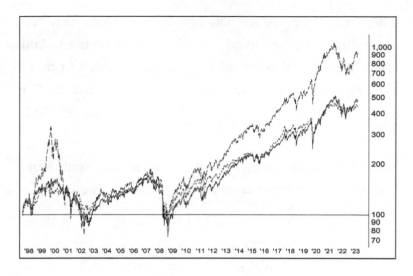

FIGURE 8: DOW VERSUS S&P 500 VERSUS NASDAQ

Source: FactSet data and analytics

markets goes way back, so much so that it is unclear how or when it started.

A bull market is when traders and investors are optimistic and are generally buying stocks across the broad, thereby pushing share prices higher.

Whereas a bear market is when they are fearful or pessimistic, and broadly selling stocks, pushing prices lower.

Investor sentiment and psychology are not the only cause for bull and bear markets. Big, macro factors like interest rates, inflation, economic growth, consumer confidence, population growth, and geopolitics paint with a broad brush. They affect most companies in a similarly positive or negative way.

There are of course special, unique companies that can completely buck the trend, but they are exceptions. And even these special companies might be included in more than one index, causing correlation in the returns. For example, Apple (AAPL) is included in the Dow, the S&P 500, and the Nasdaq.

While the indexes generally move in tandem, their absolute and relative performance varies from time to time.

Since the Dow comprises stable, blue-chip-type companies, it tends to outperform in down markets. Whereas, the Nasdaq, with its high-flying tech companies tends to outperform in up markets.

Most assessments of the long-term returns of the U.S. stock market look at the S&P 500. The index includes enough stocks to be representative of the market, and the data goes back quite far. While the S&P 500 as we know it today dates back to 1957, the S&P index itself actually goes back to 1926, when it was created as a composite index tracking 90 stocks.

Piecing together the historical S&P data, the average annualized return since its inception in 1926 through December 31, 2022, was 9.82%. The average annualized return since becoming a 500-stock index in 1957 was 10.15%.

While a roughly 10% return per year sounds nice, it doesn't come easy. In most years the stock market does not return a clean, stress-free 10%. It is a roller coaster ride to arrive at that destination, which includes gut-wrenching pullbacks that can test the conviction of even the most disciplined long-term investors.

The average annual drawdown in the S&P 500 index historically has been 14%.

A drawdown is how far prices fall from a peak before bottoming and beginning to rise again.

A 14% average drawdown for the S&P 500 means that even though stocks have grinded higher over time, investors have on average had to see the value of their investments drop by 14% each year. There were several drawdowns in excess of 30% and even one close to 50%.

It's one thing to acknowledge that reality. It's another to live it.

When your hard-earned savings and your retirement nest egg plummet in value, it requires conviction and emotional control to remain invested.

For those who were able to weather the volatility and ride it out over several decades, it turned out to be an attractive 10% per year average return.

You may think, but how much of that return was just driven by inflation?

The U.S. dollar has lost over 90% of its purchasing power in the last 100 years. The natural question is: is the stock market generating real wealth or just keeping up with a declining dollar?

The answer is pretty clear that investing in the stock market has generated **real returns**—that is, returns adjusted for inflation.

Adjusted for measured inflation, the average annual real return of stocks has been around 7%.

We get that by taking the 10% average nominal return and subtracting 3%, which is the average annual inflation rate in the U.S. over the past 90 years.

So, even accounting for inflation, it appears that stocks have generated significant real wealth over time.

For those who are skeptical of how inflation is measured, another angle in which you can view stock returns is versus gold. The precious metal has historically been considered "real money" and a hedge against inflation.

There is a saying about gold that one ounce buys a fine suit across centuries. It speaks to the stability of its purchasing power in real terms over long periods of time.

So, how have stocks fared against gold?

You can see in Figure 9 that going back to the 1970s the S&P 500 has outperformed gold by a wide margin.

If you had invested $100 in gold in 1978, it would be worth around $1,100 as of 2023. But if you had invested $100 in the S&P 500, it would be worth around $4,500, and that's not even including all the dividend payments received along the way. If you were to include reinvested dividends, the outperformance would have been even more pronounced.

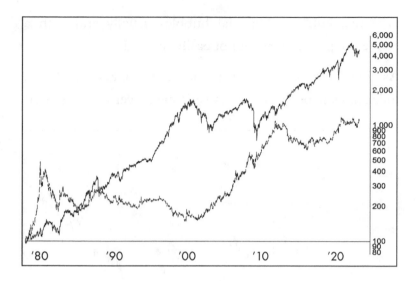

FIGURE 9: S&P 500 VERSUS GOLD—35Y

Source: FactSet data and analytics

This makes intuitive sense. The idea behind investing in stocks is that good businesses are productive and generate a real return for their owners in excess of inflation. Over time, these returns compound and produce significant wealth for investors in both real and nominal terms.

That has historically been the case for U.S. stocks. However, it is important to note that nowhere is it set in stone that stock indexes must always rise. Consider Japan, which witnessed the bursting of a stock market bubble in 1990.

A "bubble" is when the price of something rises so high based on investor sentiment and psychology that it becomes unsustainable. It is usually fueled more by excessive optimism and herd behavior than by any real change in the underlying asset.

Like real bubbles, financial bubbles usually end with a sudden pop, and they are not easily reflated.

As Figure 10 indicates, the country's Nikkei 225 Stock index has still not regained its 1990 high, over 30 years later!

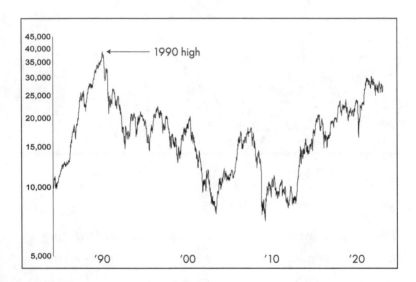

FIGURE 10: NIKKEI 225—35Y

Source: FactSet data and analytics

The U.S. stock market experienced a significant correction in 2022 following a manic, bubble-like rally in 2020 and 2021. Only time will tell if and when the long-term uptrend resumes.

The beginnings and ends of market corrections are very difficult to forecast.

During each correction, you will hear of the prescient individuals who predicted the downturn. But keep in mind, those people who got it right might have been predicting the collapse every year for the last two decades. They were bound to be right eventually!

In hindsight, there is usually a reason attached to the correction that seems somewhat obvious. However, at the time, you never know how an event will play out or how the stock market will respond to it.

You can see on the chart of the S&P 500 in Figure 11 that, in hindsight, a reason can be attributed to all the major corrections of the past 25 years.

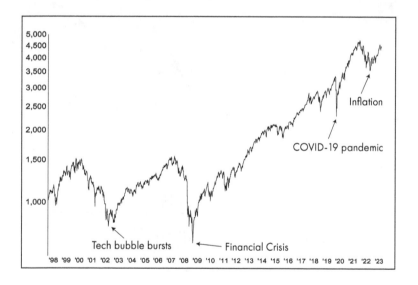

FIGURE 11: S&P 500—25Y

Source: FactSet data and analytics

A bubble in technology stocks caused the 2001 correction, a financial crisis caused the 2008 correction, Covid-19 caused the 2020 correction, inflation and the Russia/Ukraine war caused the 2022 correction.

It is only in hindsight that we see how these issues were resolved and how the markets recovered.

These momentary pullbacks can be quite significant. However, if you take a longer-term view and zoom out far enough on a chart of the S&P 500, as in Figure 12, the pullbacks start to appear less significant, and the clear trend is a diagonal line higher.

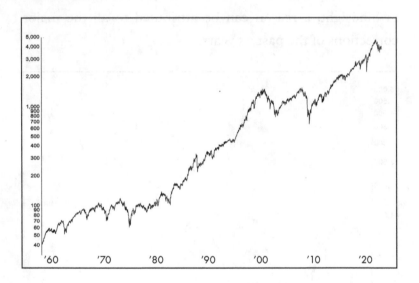

FIGURE 12: S&P 500–65Y

Source: FactSet data and analytics

The volatility in individual stocks is even greater than it is for indexes. A basket of stocks will smooth out the extremes and yield an average, but anything can happen to a single company.

Even some of the best-performing stocks experience big drawdowns over their lifetimes.

Consider Apple (AAPL), which over the last 30 years has become one of the most iconic and successful companies in the world. If you invested $1,000 in AAPL in 1990, it would be worth over $500,000 in 2023.

That's a life-changing return, but it didn't come easy. Apple shares had several drawdowns in excess of 30% over those years. In fact, investors even had to weather two separate drawdowns of more than 80%, one from 1991 to 1997 and another from 2000 to 2003.

The stock market can be a dangerous ride for those who don't stay strapped in.

If you watch financial media, they will broadcast the screaming and yelling at every twist and turn. It can be difficult not to react emotionally.

There has always been volatility in stock prices and there always will be. It is the nature of uncertainty, and of risk and reward.

A common measure of how much volatility there is in the market at any given time is the **volatility index**, known as the **VIX**.

The VIX is derived from the prices of S&P 500 index options with near-term expiration dates. It is essentially a gauge for how far stock prices are expected to move in the next 30 days.

When the VIX is high, there is usually a lot of uncertainty in the market and prices are moving fast.

When the VIX is low, there is usually relative calm in the markets and prices are not making sudden or drastic moves.

A high VIX is usually associated with a pullback in the market. A common saying is that a bull market takes the stairs up and the elevator down. Volatility—panic—usually arises when prices are falling.

In a bear market, which is generally defined as a prolonged fall in stock prices where the major indexes fall by 20% or more from their previous highs, volatility can reach extremes.

Figure 13 shows a 20-year chart of the VIX from 2003 to 2023. You can see that extreme measures, above 50, were reached during periods of extreme fear—during the Financial Crisis in 2008–2009 and the Covid-19 pandemic in early 2020.

These two periods ended up being the two best buying opportunities of those two decades.

If you swam against the current and bought stocks during these periods when the VIX was high, and held them until the panic subsided, you'd have made out extraordinarily well.

As the legendary Warren Buffett famously said, investors should be "fearful when others are greedy, and greedy when others are fearful."

Historically, it has paid to take the other side of public emotion.

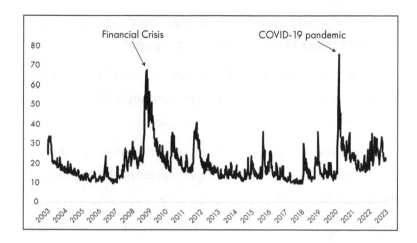

FIGURE 13: CBOE VOLATILITY INDEX "THE VIX"
Source: Yahoo! Finance

EXCHANGE TRADED FUNDS (ETFs)

The major stock indexes provide good representations of the broader stock market, but can you invest in them?

The answer is yes. You can do it easily through what's called an **exchange traded fund**, or **ETF**.

ETFs have become a huge force in equity markets.

As of 2022, ETFs had come to account for about a third of the total dollar volume traded in the stock market each day.

ETFs were a revolutionary product when they were introduced in the 1990s, because they gave investors the ability to purchase a diversified group of stocks under a single instrument (product) without having to pay a hefty expense fee to a professional fund manager.

An ETF is like a basket. In the same way that you can buy or sell a share of an individual company, an ETF allows you to buy or sell a basket of many companies.

The creation of an ETF involves a financial company, known as a sponsor, who buys stocks that represent the holdings of the basket they wish to create.

It can be anything—the basket might include the 500 stocks in the S&P 500, or it might include only oil & gas companies or only biotechnology companies. The combinations are endless. The ETF basket is essentially any combination of stocks that the sponsor believes would make for an attractive product for investors.

Once the desired stocks are purchased, the shares are put into a trust, and the sponsor issues ETF shares that represent the value of the portfolio of these holdings. The ETF shares are then made available on the open market, where buyers and sellers can trade them as they wish.

Many of the most popular ETFs track the major stock indexes, like the Dow, the S&P 500, or the Nasdaq Composite.

An investment in an ETF that tracks an index is considered a **passive investment**, meaning there is no professional investor constantly evaluating the basket and changing the stocks in it based on their opinion. The basket is predetermined, and it remains the same unless there is a change made to the index that it was created to track, in which case the ETF would be appropriately adjusted.

Passive investing is in contrast to **active investing**, or active management, in which a professional investor is paid to manage a portfolio of stocks, buying and selling them according to their own determinations.

As decades of data on stock pickers started to compile, the evidence increasingly indicated that the highly paid, professional portfolio managers did not on average produce better returns for investors than what would have been achieved by simply passively investing in an index.

For many investors, ETFs seemed to offer equal or better returns at a fraction of the cost. It was a no-brainer.

ETFs are also very user friendly in that they trade on an exchange with a ticker symbol and can be bought and sold throughout the day just like a normal stock.

ETFs are very accessible to individual investors. The big, well-known leaders in the space like Vanguard and BlackRock offer many different passive ETFs tracking most of the major indexes.

Their websites provide descriptions of each ETF offered, along with the ticker symbol that can be used to purchase them through any broker.

Table 5 shows the ten largest stock ETFs by assets, as of 2023.

TABLE 5: LARGEST STOCK ETFs

TICKER SYMBOL	NAME	ASSETS UNDER MANAGEMENT (AUM)	DESCRIPTION
SPY	SPDR S&P 500 ETF Trust	$426,306,000.00	Tracks the S&P 500 index (500 of the biggest U.S. companies)
IVV	iShares Core S&P 500 ETF	$348,519,000.00	Tracks the S&P 500 index
VOO	Vanguard S&P 500 ETF	$335,346,000.00	Tracks the S&P 500 index
VTI	Vanguard Total Stock Market ETF	$319,720,000.00	Tracks the Total U.S. Stock Market index (all U.S. companies)
QQQ	Invesco QQQ Trust Series I	$214,173,000.00	Tracks the Nasdaq 100 index (big tech companies)
VEA	Vanguard FTSE Developed Markets ETF	$117,041,000.00	Tracks the FTSE Developed All Cap ex U.S. Index (companies in Canada, Europe, and the Pacific, but excluding U.S. companies)
IEFA	iShares Core MSCI EAFE ETF	$101,621,000.00	Tracks a basket of developed market equities, excluding the U.S. and Canada
VTV	Vanguard Value ETF	$100,958,000.00	Tracks the performance of the CRSP U.S. Large Cap Value Index (U.S. value stocks)
VUG	Vanguard Growth ETF	$96,280,900.00	Tracks the performance of the CRSP U.S. Large Cap Growth Index (U.S. growth stocks)
VWO	Vanguard FTSE Emerging Markets ETF	$74,708,100.00	Tracks companies located in emerging markets around the world, such as China, Brazil, Taiwan, and South Africa

You will notice that there is crossover in the ETF world, with many firms offering similar ETFs. This is especially true for ETFs that track the major indexes, such as the S&P 500, which is where there is the most investor demand.

In recent years, ETFs of all kinds from many different sponsors have come to the market. There are ETFs available for nearly all sectors, like energy, financials, industrials, consumer discretionary, etc. There are also ETFs for different themes and investing styles, like innovative growth or dividend value.

I even noticed that there is now an ETF that tracks the inverse of the popular CNBC market commentator Jim Cramer's trade ideas. Perhaps it's a sign that ETFs have gone too far!

Some ETFs are also creeping back toward active management. The line between passive, index-tracking ETFs and actively managed mutual funds is getting blurrier.

Some actively managed ETFs have attracted both media and investor attention, like Cathie Wood's ARK Innovation Fund, which generated massive returns following the Covid-19 outbreak in 2020 only to give back all the gains by the spring of 2022.

History Lesson: the beginning of ETFs

John Bogel's Vanguard is widely credited with introducing ETFs to the masses.

The first step toward ETFs as we now know them came from Wells Fargo and American National Bank, which both launched index mutual funds in 1973 for

---

institutional customers. These funds were created in response to academic research that was beginning to indicate that passive investing might have advantages over actively managed funds.

John Bogle had strong conviction in the idea of passive investing. Despite receiving some criticism at the time, he launched the first public index mutual fund on December 31, 1975. It was called the First Index Investment Trust and it tracked the S&P 500 index.

Interest in passive index investing grew steadily, but it wasn't until 1993 that the first ETF was brought to market. State Street Global Investors was the pioneer, releasing the S&P 500 Trust ETF, called SPDR or "spider," on January 22, 1993. It trades under the ticker symbol SPY, and it remains one of the most actively traded ETFs to this day.

While John Bogel championed the idea of passive index investing, he was at first not a fan of the ETF product. He believed in long-term investing, and he worried that the all-day access of ETFs would turn them into short-term trading vehicles. He preferred the index mutual fund structure, which priced funds at the end of the day and could not be traded during normal market hours, which he thought would promote better behavior.

Vanguard eventually came around to ETFs and began offering them in 2001, but only after Bogel no longer played a leading role at the firm. It has worked out well for Vanguard. They now have nearly $2trn in ETF assets under management, second only to BlackRock.

Now we understand the major stock indexes, how they've historically performed, and how people invest in them.

In the next chapter, we highlight the intermediaries through which most individuals participate in the stock market: brokers, wealth managers, and robo-advisors.

CHAPTER 13:
INTERACTING WITH
THE STOCK MARKET

YOUR FRIEND TELLS you that he is invested in the
stock market.

That means he owns stocks, but how is he actually interacting
with the stock market? Is he submitting his own orders? Is
he paying someone else to invest for him?

In the United States there are four common avenues through
which individuals invest in the stock market: online brokers,
wealth managers, robo-advisors, and employer sponsored
retirement plans.

Each of these avenues serves a different need. Some
individuals will invest through a combination of several or
all of them.

ONLINE BROKERS

Individual investors don't show up on the floor of the New York Stock Exchange to submit orders.

Instead, they place orders through a licensed broker, which is an individual or a firm that acts as an intermediary between an investor and a securities exchange.

Before the internet age, investors would have to call a licensed broker and pay a hefty commission for the broker to place their trade. But as with many areas of life, technology has lowered costs and streamlined the process.

Online brokers, also known as discount brokers, were made possible by the internet. They will execute trades on behalf of a client for a low cost, but they don't typically provide investment advice.

Online brokers are great for the do-it-yourself investor.

They allow for simple and cheap trade execution, and they provide all the necessary forms and documents required for taxes or other purposes.

As an investor, when you log into the online broker's website you'll see a homepage with an account value, similar to what you'd see with a normal checking or savings account. Only, with a brokerage account, you can buy and sell stocks and other securities, and your account value will continuously fluctuate as the market prices of your investments change.

The brokerage account gets linked with a bank account so that you can deposit and withdraw cash as needed.

Online brokers offer customer support services, but unless you seck them out, you will likely never hear from an actual person.

You are on your own in terms of making decisions and placing orders to buy and sell shares. We discussed the order submitting process earlier in Chapter 11.

At the time of this writing, the four biggest online brokerages in terms of customers and assets are Charles Schwab, Fidelity Investments, E*TRADE, and TD Ameritrade.

During the Covid-19 outbreak in 2020, when stocks were moving higher and there were no sporting events to gamble on, an online broker called Robinhood attracted a lot of young customers who became drawn to stock and cryptocurrency trading. It became a popular broker among Millennials and Gen Z. It's too early to tell whether it was a temporary fad or the emergence of another powerful name in the space.

WEALTH MANAGERS

Understandably, not everyone wants to manage their own investments. There is a lot at stake.

For those who want human help in managing their investments, there are full-service brokers that offer wealth management services.

Wealth management is a comprehensive service. It involves more than just executing buy and sell orders.

A wealth manager takes a holistic view of one's financial circumstances. They can assist in asset allocation, tax loss harvesting, and other portfolio management services that are specific to an individual.

A good wealth management firm will develop a relationship with you. They will assign you a financial advisor, who is a person that you will hopefully come to know and trust.

While investing through an online broker can feel like being alone on an island, investing with a good financial advisor can feel like having an expert on speed dial. It is someone you can meet with and make important decisions through two-way conversation.

Oftentimes the costliest investing mistakes are the result of emotionally driven decisions. For some people, having a professional to lean on both intellectually and emotionally can be well worth the cost.

In the U.S., wealth managers are usually **registered investment advisors** (**RIAs**), which have a fiduciary responsibility to their client.

Be wary of wealth managers who work for commission or don't claim to have a fiduciary responsibility. Excess and unnecessary trading in an account, called **churn**, has been a major issue in the financial world for a long-time. This is when your broker or advisor makes changes to your portfolio because they get compensated on the commission generated by the trades. Churn is often costly and not in the best interest of the client.

Ultimately, it's your money and your financial advisor must abide by your wishes. If they fail to carry out your instructions in an accurate and timely manner, and you incur financial loss from it, you have legal recourse to seek damages, fees, and costs stemming from those losses.

There are lots of wealth management providers to choose from. It is a competitive industry where big banks like Morgan Stanley, J.P. Morgan, and Bank of New York Mellon manage a lot of money, but there are also a lot of boutique firms that offer exceptional services.

If you have concerns about your treatment at one firm, you can always switch to another one.

Breaking up can seem hard to do. The process of switching brokers might feel overwhelming, but be assured, it is relatively straightforward.

Once you've selected the new firm you'd like to work with, they will have you complete a **transfer initiation form (TIF)**. After the TIF is completed and returned, it will take several days for the assets to transfer, but it is mostly an automated back-office procedure between your new and old brokers. From the client's perspective, it is not an onerous ordeal.

Stock investments can be transferred as they are. No liquidation and repurchasing of the stocks is required, so there do not have to be tax implications from the switching of brokers.

ROBO-ADVISORS

In the last 15 years a new phenomenon has arisen: **robo-advisors**.

Robo-advisors are a cross between do-it-yourself online brokers and full-service wealth managers.

A robo-advisor won't buy or sell individual stocks for you. For that you will still need a broker.

They are also not known for developing the personal relationships provided by full-service wealth managers.

Where robo-advisors have found their niche is in portfolio construction.

They have automated the investment process. For a significantly lower fee, a robo-advisor will invest your money in a way that closely mimics how a human professional would do it.

Not all human financial advisors invest the same way, but there is a general consensus on what constitutes a well-diversified, age-appropriate portfolio.

For example, if you are 30 years old, single, and employed, and want to start investing your money for the future, a traditional wealth manager might help you construct a portfolio that consists of 70% stocks and 30% bonds. They might arrive at this conclusion after speaking with you and getting to know your age, financial circumstances, and risk tolerance.

A robo-advisor uses technology to remove the human advisor from the process. Instead of having a discussion with a person, you'll answer a few standard questions on the robo-advisor's website or app about age, income, goals, and so on. Based on your responses, they will generate an asset allocation and portfolio that is often very similar to what a human financial advisor would have recommended.

The robo-advisor is not a stock picker. It does not do analysis or have opinions on individual stocks.

The key to its being able to offer a low-cost, diversified portfolio is through the use of ETFs, which as we discussed in the previous chapter, are low-cost funds that passively track a broader basket of stocks.

The robo-advisor will invest in a series of ETFs to achieve the desired exposures and diversification.

The automated process plus the use of low-cost ETFs allows these companies to offer a discounted wealth management service. The fees are higher than what you'd pay by doing everything yourself through an online broker, but they are lower than what you'd pay for using a traditional wealth manager.

Robo-advisors can be a good middle-ground option for someone who doesn't want to manage their own investments but also doesn't want to pay the fees for full-fledged support.

The robo-advisor space is still young, with the first launches having come out of the financial crisis in 2008–2010. At the time of this writing, two of the emerging leaders in the space in the U.S. are Betterment and Wealthfront.

Wealth management is a highly competitive market, and these emerging companies will run up against legacy behemoths, so it will be interesting to see how the market share war unfolds.

RETIREMENT FUNDS

The government wants to incentivize saving for retirement, so there are a number of government-sanctioned retirement plans available in the U.S.

The most commonly used is the employer-sponsored **401(k) plan**, which allows employees to save and invest pre-tax income for retirement.

By saving pre-tax dollars, the idea is that employees can put aside more money and allow it to compound over time. Taxes are due when the individual begins drawing on the funds in retirement, at which point, his or her income bracket should be lower if they've retired from work.

Individuals who invest via a 401(k) plan don't typically interact with the people who are investing their money. Instead, a third-party employment services company usually acts as a liaison between the employee's company and the asset managers who invest the 401(k) funds.

The employee decides the percentage of their paycheck that they'd like to save for retirement, and they select an investment manager from a list of a few featured funds. These funds are often mutual funds managed by prominent asset managers, including firms like Fidelity, T. Rowe Price, and Vanguard, among many others.

After the initial decision is made, usually shortly after starting a new job, many 401(k) investors pay little to no attention to how their money is being invested.

It is collectively a huge sum of money that gets funneled to asset managers on autopilot.

As of 2021 data, 401(k) plans held over $7trn dollars in assets, representing nearly one-fifth of the $37trn+ U.S. retirement market.

Some of the other common retirement plans in the U.S. include individual retirement accounts (IRAs), Roth IRAs, and simplified employee pension (SEP) IRAs, as well as pension plans, which have become less common with private employers but are still available to many public sector employees.

Now we understand the ways in which most individual investors interact with the stock market.

In the next chapter, we discuss two equity derivatives that are used by some more tactical traders and investment professionals: stock options and futures.

CHAPTER 14:
OPTIONS & FUTURES

MOST ORDINARY INVESTORS will never need to trade an options or futures contract.

Some people have made a lot of money trading them, while many more have lost money trading them.

If you are an individual using stocks to build wealth over time, you can rest assured that you do not need to experiment with these two financial products.

That said, they do serve a role for some equity traders and professional money managers. They are also often talked about in financial media and in professional financial circles, so having a general understanding of their use helps round out one's knowledge of the stock market.

OPTIONS

Your friend takes you into his dingy basement and dusts off an old shoebox. Inside are several mint condition Michael Jordan rookie cards.

"I think this box of cards might be worth about $10,000," he says.

"I think they could be worth much more than that," you reply. "Maybe $20,000!"

"I would be happy to get $10,000 for them," says your friend.

You pause and think about it. You are tempted to buy the box of cards from him for $10,000 because you think they could be sold somewhere else for $20,000. But $10,000 is just too much money to shell out.

So you make a proposition to your friend. "If I give you $500 now, will you give me the right to purchase this box from you for $10,000? I will let you know within the next month if I am going to buy the box from you. If I decide not to buy it, you can keep the $500."

"Sure, that's fine with me. You have a deal!" he says.

You give your friend the $500, and then you spend the next few weeks speaking with card collectors. Sure enough, you find one that will pay $20,000 for the box of Michael Jordan rookie cards.

Excited, you go back to your friend's house. You give him $10,000, and he gives you the box of cards.

You then immediately drive the box over to the card collector and sell it to him for $20,000.

You just made a big profit on the expensive box of cards without having fully assumed the risk of owning them.

That's because all you paid for was an *option* to buy them.

WHAT ARE OPTIONS?

A whole book could be written on options, so we will only highlight the basics here.

Options can be used in many different ways for many different purposes, from hedging risk, to generating income, to pure speculating. Options strategies run the gamut from simple to complex.

An **option** is a contract that grants its owner the right, but not the obligation, to buy or sell a specific quantity of an underlying asset at a specified strike price on or before a specified date.

The definition itself sounds complicated, but don't worry, we will break it down.

Options contracts apply to several different asset classes, including, stocks, commodities, and currencies. We will focus here only on stock options.

At the most basic level, there are two main types of options: **calls** and **puts**.

Calls give the owner of the contract the right to *buy* a stock at a specific price on or before a particular date.

Puts give the owner of the contract the right to *sell* a stock at a specific price on or before a particular date.

One options contract, either call or put, commands 100 shares of the underlying stock. The buyer of one call option has the right to purchase 100 shares of the underlying stock. And the buyer of one put option has the right to sell 100 shares of the underlying stock.

Options boil down to three things: price, premium, and time.

The focus is the share price. If you're buying an option on Apple (AAPL) stock, it's because you have a view on where the price of Apple shares are headed. The **strike price** is the price at which the owner of the option is entitled to buy or sell the underlying stock.

Nothing is free. If you want to buy the option to purchase AAPL shares at, say $150 per share, you'll have to pay a small **premium** for that right. Think of it like a fee.

And nothing lasts forever. The options contract has an **expiration date**, which is the date on which the deal expires and is no longer valid. The expiration date is usually in terms of weeks or months, but in some cases can be longer than a year.

Just as there is a market for shares of stocks, there is a separate market for stock options, where buyers and sellers make bids and offers on call and put options across different stocks.

Let's start with an example of a call option to illustrate how they work.

BUYING A CALL OPTION

Imagine that you have a hunch that the pharmaceutical company Merck (MRK) is going to get approval for a new drug that will send its stock soaring within the next three months.

The stock is currently trading at $85 on January 1, but you think by April 1 it could be worth well above $100.

You want to make a bet that the big price move occurs, but you don't want to shell out the cash to buy a lot of shares, so you decide to buy an option.

Let's say you purchase one call option at a $100 strike price for a $2 per share premium that expires on April 1.

Keep in mind, an options contract is for 100 shares of stock, so if the premium is $2 per single share, you'll have to pay $200 per one hundred shares. That means that you will pay $200 now. This can be thought of as a non-refundable down payment.

If you're right, and before April 1 MRK announces a new drug approval and the price of the stock soars to $120, then you can exercise your option to purchase 100 shares at $100.

You only risked $200, but you've made $1,800.

How does that math work?

You paid $100 per share for the stock, plus $2 per share for the option, which equates to a cost basis of $102 per share.

But the stock is now trading at $120 per share in the market at the time you exercise the option, so if you sell the shares for $120 each, you will profit $18 per share ($120 – $102) on 100 shares, which equals $1,800.

That's if your prediction was correct. But options are tricky because you not only need to be right about the price move, but also about the timing.

When you are betting on a stock to make a big move in a short, specific period of time, the odds are against you. It is very difficult to predict the short-term price movements in stocks.

In this case, if your bet is wrong and the stock does not rally past the $100 strike price, your option will expire worthless. You will lose the entire $200 premium you paid for it.

Options provide an investor with **leverage**, meaning that a relatively small down payment can result in a big percentage gain or loss.

In this case, profiting $1,800 off a $200 investment is a 900% return. You are very unlikely to generate that type of return by simply purchasing a stock and holding it, unless you hold it for a very long time.

However, there is no reward without corresponding risk. In this example, there was a high probability that the $200 down payment would be lost. That would have equated to a 100% loss on the trade.

If you instead invested the $200 in common shares of a quality company, it is unlikely that you would have lost all your money in such a short period of time.

SELLING A CALL OPTION

For every buyer of an option there is also a seller. Who might want to sell a call option?

Imagine that, instead of wanting to bet that Merck's drug would get approved and the stock would rally, you are a long-term investor in MRK who had a big chunk of your net worth invested in the stock.

You have no intention of selling it. You are hoping to hold MRK shares for a long time, and you recognize that by selling call options to the people who want to make near-term gambles, you can oftentimes pocket the money that they're willing to risk.

You see a chance to have your cake and eat it too.

You hope to generate strong returns from dividends and capital gains in MRK shares over the long-run, and as you go, you can collect periodic bonus payments from selling call options against your investment.

What's the downside?

If MRK experiences an abnormally strong rally, like in the first case to $120, then you would leave some money on the table because you would be forced to sell your shares at $100.

Stocks sometimes trade sideways for a long time only to burst higher over a short period of time. It can be frustrating and counterproductive for a long-term investor to miss out on the big moves.

BUYING A PUT OPTION

Puts work in a similar way to call options, but in reverse. If you buy one put option, you get the right to *sell* 100 shares of the underlying stock.

Let's say that, instead of thinking that Merck's drug would get approved, and the stock would rally, you thought that their drug would not receive approval and the stock would fall. In this case, you might purchase a put.

The stock is currently trading at $85 on January 1, but you think by April 1 it could be well below $75.

Let's say you purchase one put option at a $75 strike price for a $2 per share premium that expires on April 1.

That means that you will pay $200 now ($2 per share x 100 shares), which again is similar to a non-refundable down payment.

If you're right and before April 1 MRK announces that its new drug did not receive FDA approval, and the price of the stock craters to $60, then you can exercise your option to sell 100 shares at $75.

Since the stock is now trading below where you are entitled to sell it, your puts are "in the money," which is a phrase used to describe when an options contract could be exercised for a profit.

In this trade, you only risked $200, but you've made $1,300.

How does that math work?

You had purchased the right to sell 100 shares at $75 per share, and the stock is now trading in the market for only $60. You can make an instant $15 per share by selling the 100 shares at $75 and buying them back for $60.

But remember, you paid $2 per share to purchase the option, so you have to subtract that from your true earnings. That leaves you with a profit of $13 per share on 100 shares, which equals $1,300.

Like with call options, the high-risk, high-reward nature of the returns makes them an attractive product for speculators.

It should be noted, though, that speculation is not the only purpose of put options.

For instance, perhaps the long-term owner of MRK shares is worried about a potential selloff in the stock, so he might decide to purchase puts as protection. He could pay a small premium for a put option to lock in a sale price for his stock, almost like paying for an insurance policy in case something goes wrong.

SELLING A PUT OPTION

Again, for every buyer of an option there is a seller.

If you sell a put, you are giving someone else the right to sell shares. That means that you, the seller of the put option, would have to buy the shares if the stock falls below the exercise price.

This could make sense for someone who wants to purchase a particular stock but only if it pulls back to a lower price than where it's currently trading.

For example, if MRK shares are trading at $85 and you would be willing to buy them at $75, you could sell a put at $75 and collect a premium for selling the option.

It could potentially be a win-win setup.

If the stock trades below $75, you'll have to buy the shares, but you wanted to buy them anyway.

And if the stock doesn't fall to $75, well, you just keep the payment you received for selling the put option.

As you can see, when it comes to options, the aims and intentions among buyers and sellers can vary widely.

In the stock market, options are very much a game within the game.

FUTURES

Imagine that you are a corn farmer getting ready for the spring planting.

You invest a great deal of time, money, and effort getting the seeds in the ground. You have a lot riding on the upcoming summer harvest.

You've run the numbers, and if you're not able to get $4 per bushel for your corn, you'll have lost money on the whole operation. You may not be able to pay your bills.

Wouldn't it be nice if you could lock in a profitable sale price for your corn beforehand?

If you were able to secure a profitable price, say $6 per bushel, ahead of time, you could just worry about farming and not about what the *future* price of corn will be.

That's where futures contracts come into play.

WHAT ARE FUTURES?

A **futures contract** is a legally binding agreement to buy or sell some asset at a fixed price but to be delivered and paid for later.

In your case, as the corn farmer, you might sell a corn futures contract, which would obligate you to sell a specified amount of corn for $6 per bushel.

As with options, for every seller of a futures contract there is a buyer. The buyer of the contract, in this case, would be obligated to take delivery of the corn on a specified date and pay $6 per bushel for it.

Futures are often associated with commodities, like corn, crude oil, natural gas, coffee, copper, and so on, but there are also futures contracts for stock indexes.

The most well-known and liquid stock futures contract is the **E-mini S&P 500 contract**, which trades on the Chicago Mercantile Exchange (CME) under the ticker ES.

The E-mini S&P 500 futures contract tracks the price of the S&P 500 index.

Why is it called E-mini? Originally there had been a larger S&P 500 contract that required greater capital requirements to trade it. The E-mini was offered as a smaller contract with lower capital requirements that would be more accessible to the individual trader.

The E-mini, however, became very popular and attracted all the volume, so the bigger contract was removed, and the E-mini became the main S&P 500 futures contract traded by both individuals and institutions alike.

For a commodity like corn, the buyer and seller are on the hook to take or make delivery of the actual, physical commodity. The farmer delivers corn, for example. But most financial traders who participate in commodity futures markets have no intention of ever dealing with the physical commodity, so they close out their positions before the contracts expire.

If you buy a futures contract and then sell it before the specified cutoff date, called **expiration**, you cancel out your obligation and are no longer responsible for taking or making delivery of the actual commodity.

Once you have canceled out your buy order with a sell order, or vice versa, you are left with only the financial gain or loss on the trade based on the prices at which you bought and sold the contract.

With the S&P 500 futures contract, there is an expiration date but there is no delivery. It is purely a financial instrument.

When the contract expires, the shares of the 500 U.S. companies included in the S&P 500 index do not get transferred from the seller of the contract to the buyer. Instead, it is cash settled, meaning the buyer and seller of the futures contract are only on the hook for the monetary gain or loss incurred from their trade.

For example, if you purchased an S&P 500 futures contract and the value of that index proceeded to fall and expire at a lower price, you would be obligated to pay the amount of the loss in cash.

Similarly, if you bought an S&P 500 futures contract and the value of the index proceeded to rise and expire at a higher price, you would receive the profit in cash.

No actual shares of stock trade hands in the futures market.

WHY DO PEOPLE TRADE STOCK FUTURES?

People are drawn to the S&P 500 futures contract for different reasons.

There are always speculators, and there is no better place to get a gambling bang for your buck than the futures market. In the futures market, traders are only required to front a fraction of the contract's actual value, known as **margin**.

The low margin requirements allow traders to command big sums of money with only a relatively small account balance. This makes for a high-risk, high-reward game because the profit and loss on trades can become multiples of the initial investment.

It is possible to make a fortune in the futures market, but you can also lose everything, including more than the amount deposited in your account.

For example, if you short an S&P 500 futures contract and it keeps moving higher in price, your loss could start to exceed your cash balance. You will receive a **margin call** from your broker, demanding that you deposit more money in the account.

While some individuals are surely attracted to the high stakes gambling aspect of the futures market, there are others, especially institutions, who use it to hedge risk.

For example, a portfolio manager might own a well-constructed portfolio of stocks, but disturbing news breaks at night that makes her concerned about the market. She might sell S&P 500 futures as a hedge against her individual stock investments. This way, if the market opens down big in the morning, the gains from her S&P 500 short position might offset some of the losses on her stock holdings.

The market open is itself a reason why S&P 500 index futures attract a lot of attention.

The official hours of the major U.S. stock exchanges are from 9:30am to 4:00pm Eastern Standard Time. Of course, the world does not go to sleep when the market closes.

S&P 500 futures trade around the clock except for a 30-minute settlement period after the close, so people will watch the futures market as an indicator for how stocks will open in the morning.

If you check where the market is trading at night or in the early morning, you will see a quote that's based on the futures market. CNBC and other financial media outlets will show an "implied open" quote, which is a real-time estimate of where the S&P 500 market index would open based on the current price of the S&P 500 futures contract.

Financial media outlets will also typically show the implied open for the Dow Jones Industrial Average and the Nasdaq Composite indexes.

Extended-hours trading

While there are no futures contracts for individual stocks, there is **after-hours trading** beyond the official 9:30am to 4:00pm ET market hours.

When the closing bell at the New York Stock Exchange rings at 4:00pm, the primary exchanges are closed, but traders can still place orders through electronic communication networks, or ECNs, which we described in Chapter 10. After-hours trading takes place from the 4:00pm close to about 8:00pm ET.

After-hours trading is not limited to industry insiders. Non-professional investors can access after-hours through some platforms. However, the fees are typically higher than what would be associated with trades placed during normal market hours.

Liquidity drops off substantially in the after-market and becomes very thin by 8:00pm ET. Bid-ask spreads can become wide because all the big, market-making players have shut down for the day.

Pre-market trading is like after-hours trading except it takes place in the morning. Pre-market trading takes place from 4:00am to 9:30am ET, depending on the platform.

Now you are familiar with options and futures—the games within the game.

In the next and final chapter, we discuss mergers and acquisitions (M&A), a topic that gets a lot of media attention because it can not only affect stock prices, but it can alter the competitive landscape of industries.

CHAPTER 15: MERGERS AND ACQUISITIONS (M&A)

MERGERS AND ACQUISITIONS (M&A) are exciting!

M&A not only make individual stock prices move, but they can also have real-world competitive implications.

A merger is when two or more companies join together to form one new company. It is usually done on friendly terms, as the companies see an opportunity to mutually benefit by coming together.

A merger may help the companies more efficiently share technology, information, and resources, and it may strengthen their overall competitive position in their market.

A high-profile example of a merger was when Exxon Corp. and Mobil Corp.—the first- and second-largest oil producers in the United States—merged together to form ExxonMobil in 1998. The two companies were fine on their own, but together they were even stronger.

There were several reasons for the merger, but one of the main ones was that by joining together the combined company would have a stronger global presence and be better able to compete with big international players in the oil market.

An acquisition is somewhat different. It is when a financially stronger company acquires more than 50% of a less strong company's shares in order to take ownership of it. Acquisitions are sometimes accomplished on friendly terms, but not always.

There are many reasons why one company may want to acquire another company, including gaining new markets or new customers, or reducing competition.

A good example of a successful strategic acquisition was when Facebook (now Meta) acquired Instagram in 2012. At the time, many people thought CEO Mark Zuckerberg was making a mistake by paying a hefty $1bn for the young social media app.

Mr. Zuckerberg, however, recognized that not only did Instagram pose a significant competitive threat to Facebook's business, but that under Facebook's ownership that threat could be turned into a huge opportunity. He ended up being right. Ten years later, Instagram has over two billion users and is one of the most profitable social media platforms in the world.

When word of a potential merger or acquisition breaks, the stock prices of the companies involved can react quickly.

Typically, a business being acquired is purchased for a premium to its current market price, so investors will often bid up the potential acquiree in anticipation of a deal.

Almost immediately, if the bid rumor is credible, the stock will trade up to a level somewhat close to the rumored takeout price. It usually won't trade all the way there because the deal isn't official yet, and there is always risk that it will fall through for regulatory or other reasons.

The **Federal Trade Commission (FTC)** must approve mergers and acquisitions. They are keen to strike down M&A that might create monopolies or anticompetitive industries that could harm consumers.

For example, in 2011 the telecommunications giant AT&T tried to acquire T-Mobile USA Inc., but regulators ruled that the deal was not in the public's interest. They claimed that by eliminating a key competitor in the mobile phone market, subscription fees were likely to rise, and the remaining providers would have less incentive to improve services.

When the government stands opposed to a merger or acquisition, it can be a costly legal battle to fight back. In many cases, the potential acquirer and acquiree will drop the deal, as was the case with AT&T and T-Mobile USA.

Regulatory hurdles are not the only thing standing in the way of mergers and acquisitions. Sometimes the issue comes down to valuation or financing.

When news broke in January 2022 that two private equity firms had made bids to purchase the American retailer Kohl's (KSS), the stock shot up 36% that day.

The bids were said to be around $64–$65 per share. Over the next couple weeks, the stock traded in the high $50s to low $60s as the market assessed the probability of a deal happening.

The Kohl's management team did not want to sell. They expressed publicly that they were open to all avenues for creating value for their shareholders, but they believed that even at $64–$65 per share the market was significantly undervaluing the business.

Over the next few months, the broader stock market took a nosedive due to macroeconomic reasons, and many companies saw their share prices fall significantly. While Kohl's took time weighing its options and hoping for a higher-priced offer, the selloff in the stock market made the potential acquirers think twice about their original offers.

Simultaneously, as the stock market weakened, interest rates were rising, and speculation began that banks would not finance a big acquisition in the deteriorating market environment.

Kohl's shares had run into a perfect storm. By the end of June, the company announced that they had abandoned sale talks and the stock fell into the low $30s, a massive fall from the $64–$65 that had been offered just a few months earlier (see Figure 14).

As the saying goes, a bird in the hand is worth two in the bush.

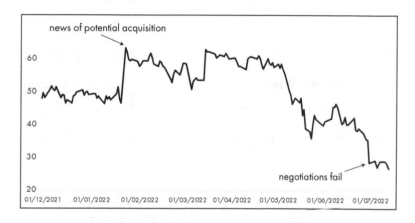

FIGURE 14: KOHL'S (KSS) PRICE CHART

Source: FactSet data and analytics

Kohl's is a relatively small retailer that sells ubiquitous, discretionary items like clothes, shoes, and home and kitchen products. Had the company been acquired, it probably would not have had far reaching implications for the rest of retail.

Sometimes, however, M&A can alter the competitive landscape of an entire industry.

Amazon, for instance, can disrupt any industry it gets into. Given its scale, its connection to customers, its technological capabilities, and its elite execution, they are an 800-pound gorilla that all companies must keep an eye on.

When Amazon acquired Whole Foods on June 16, 2017, it sent shivers into the grocery space. The fear was not only that Amazon would gobble market share from traditional grocers, but that Amazon's modern grocery model would eventually render old business models obsolete.

Those fears have not yet materialized—traditional grocers are still doing okay—but at the time, the concern was real.

On the day the Whole Foods acquisition was announced, grocery stocks took a beating.

Table 6 shows how the major grocery stocks closed that day.

TABLE 6: M&A RIPPLE EFFECTS: AMAZON BUYS WHOLE FOODS

GROCERY STOCK PRICE PERFORMANCE ON JUNE 16, 2017, THE DAY AMAZON ANNOUNCED ITS ACQUISITION OF WHOLE FOODS.	
Company	Stock price change
Whole Foods	+27%
Amazon	+2.44%
Walmart	–4.65%
Target	–5.16%
Costco	–7.19%
Kroger	–9.24%
Dollar General	–3.04%
SuperValu	–14.48%
Sprouts Market	–6.29%
Smart & Final Stores	–18.75%
Weis Markets	–4.75%
Ingles Markets	–3%

Whole Foods shareholders made out nicely, receiving $42 per share, a 27% premium to where the stock was trading prior to the announcement of the acquisition.

When an acquisition is completed, the owners of the acquired stock receive either cash or shares of the new parent company. Sometimes they receive a combination of both. In the Amazon-Whole Foods deal, Whole Foods' shareholders received cash.

If you're a student of business or you're the strategic leader of a company, or somewhere in between, reviewing the successes and failures of past mergers and acquisitions can be quite insightful. There are many M&A case studies that can be found online or in business textbooks.

As an investor, you very well may encounter the effects of M&A, either directly via share price reactions or indirectly via competitive changes to industries, but it is probably best not to speculate on it.

There are too many unknowns and moving pieces to make it worth trying to bet on which companies will be taken over.

INSIDER TRADING

The quick profit from owning a company that gets acquired can make it tempting for those in the know to trade on secretive information.

Think about how many people must have some knowledge of an acquisition before it gets announced to the public. There are insiders at both companies assessing whether the deal makes sense. During their assessment, they might consult with accountants, analysts, lawyers, and so on. And all those people have friends, family, and colleagues. Information can easily spill.

There are strict rules against trading on this type of inside information, enforced by the SEC.

The line between acceptable and unacceptable behavior can be blurry, but you kind of know it when you see it.

If your friend loves to listen to music on Spotify and tells you to buy shares because he thinks the company will be acquired—feel free to buy it. He's just giving an opinion. He doesn't know anything.

But, on the other hand, if your friend is a senior executive at Spotify and tells you to buy shares because they are going to accept a takeover bid—don't do it. That would be trading on non-public information. It would qualify as **insider trading**.

The penalties can be severe, including fines up to $5m and imprisonment for up to 20 years.

No one is immune from the law.

In 2004, television celebrity Martha Stewart was convicted of insider trading. She maintains her innocence to this day, but she made suspiciously timed trades that caught the SEC's attention. She was sentenced to five months in prison and two years of supervised release, along with a $30,000 fine.

It's best to steer clear of anything that could be construed as trading on non-public information. The risk is not worth the reward.

———

Insider trading aside, if you own a stock that gets acquired for cash, you now have capital that can be redeployed elsewhere. It's time to look for another investment opportunity!

There are always plenty of them. That is the beauty of the stock market.

CONCLUSION

I N THIS BOOK we covered companies, stocks, and the stock market.

We now know the basics of how companies are structured and how their performance is measured.

We know what stocks are, how to own them, and the mechanisms through which investors can make money in them.

And we understand the most important and relevant features of the stock market, like how and where stocks trade, and the indexes that are representative of different segments of the market.

In this book we did not evaluate or recommend any specific investment strategies. That type of information was intentionally left out because not everyone who wants or needs to understand stocks has the aim of investing.

So where do you go from here?

Whether you plan to invest or you just want to keep building your general knowledge of stocks, I would suggest trying to follow the stock market on a daily or weekly basis. You can do that by either reading about it in financially focused newspapers, blogs or newsletters, or by turning on financial television for a few minutes each day.

Just by listening and paying attention the concepts will sink in by osmosis and start to make sense over time.

It's like learning a new language: it's most effective to consistently surround yourself with people who speak it.

For those of you who do want to learn more about how to invest, there are many books and resources available.

In the pages following this conclusion, I briefly highlight my first book, *The World's Simplest Stock Picking Strategy: How to make money investing in the companies in your life*.

It describes an investing strategy that I use to invest in some of the companies that I know and use in my personal life.

To all of you, best of luck from here in your stock market journey, wherever it may take you!

MY OTHER BOOK

MY OTHER BOOK is called *The World's Simplest Stock Picking Strategy: How to make money investing in the companies in your life.*

The book describes a strategy that I personally use to invest in some of the companies that I know and use in my own life.

It is a simple, intuitive strategy for anyone who has a desire to invest in individual stocks.

Some of the best stocks have been companies that were probably right in front of you the whole time—Apple, Amazon, Google, and so on.

The World's Simplest Stock Picking Strategy guides you step by step in the process I use to keep tabs on special companies and make disciplined, long-term investments in them.

WHAT READERS HAVE SAID ABOUT *THE WORLD'S SIMPLEST STOCK PICKING STRATEGY*

"Brilliant book! It's really simple to follow, everything was so well explained and, being fairly new to the stock market, it's easily the best book I've read on investing. I can now see why I've made mistakes on investments and I'm looking forward to implementing these strategies!"

"Informative, enjoyable, and impactful to my investing journey. I will surely recommend this book to friends and family."

"I seldomly read a book in one day. I could not put your book down today and finished it. I loved it. I plan on giving three copies to my daughters as well. Once I am gone this strategy will help them immensely. Thank you for your wonderful investment guide."

"The strategy is intriguing... thanks for writing this amazing book!"

"I really enjoyed reading this book, it was insightful and fun!"

"I really loved this book and its common-sense, doable approach."

"Loved everything about this book! I will be giving a copy of the book to my young adult daughters!"

"I feel inspired by this method."

"This is the book I have been looking for the last so many years. Thanks for writing."

"A great book... gave me a new perspective on choosing good stocks and making decisions on buy/hold/sell."

"Fascinating book. Thoroughly enjoyed reading it."

"Clear, concise, simple, and easy to apply... Best book ever."

"Excellent book. I like the keep it simple approach and will be applying it."

"Great book and simple to follow."

"I really enjoyed this book and learning your process. It keeps it practical and manageable."

"I finished reading your book within a day. It's very entertaining and contains a lot of practical tips. Thanks for writing the book and sharing your knowledge."

"I recently read your book, *The World's Simplest Stock Picking Strategy*, and found it to be very insightful. I appreciate the practical advice and clear explanations you provided, which have helped me better understand how to invest in the stock market."

"I wanted to express my gratitude for writing the book *The World's Simplest Stock Pricing Strategy*. As someone who is new to investing, starting at the age of 27 may feel a bit late, but your book has been incredibly helpful in clarifying the concepts for me. I consider it to be the best stock picking strategy book I have come across. What I particularly appreciate about your book is the clear and straightforward language used throughout. It has made understanding the content much easier for me. I wanted to take a moment to thank you for writing such an informative and accessible book, and I am eager to share it with others who may benefit from it as well."

ACKNOWLEDGMENTS

I WOULD LIKE TO thank the talented team at Harriman House for all their help through the process.

Craig Pearce for helping me craft the vision for this project. Without your guidance this book would not have happened.

Nick Fletcher for editing and helping make this a much better book.

Chris Parker for the brilliant cover design.

And to the rest of the team, thank you for all the work that went into properly bringing this book to market.

ABOUT THE AUTHOR

EDWARD RYAN has spent over 15 years in institutional equity sales and proprietary trading. Edward provides investment advice to some of the world's top asset managers and has worked closely with Wall Street's top-ranked analysts in areas spanning consumer, transportation, airlines,  utilities, oil & gas, healthcare, accounting & tax policy, portfolio strategy, and quantitative investing. The portfolio he managed while trading returned 1200% over a four-year period. His first book, *The World's Simplest Stock Picking Strategy*, has been translated into six languages. When he isn't working, Edward spends time outdoors hiking, jogging, or strolling with his wife and two children. Edward holds a bachelor's degree in economics from New York University.

Printed in the USA
CPSIA information can be obtained
at www.ICGtesting.com
CBHW061907040524
7970CB00007B/9